BEYOND
OUR
MEANS

BEYOND OUR MEANS

HOW AMERICA'S LONG YEARS OF DEBT, DEFICITS AND RECKLESS BORROWING NOW THREATEN TO OVERWHELM US

Alfred L. Malabre, Jr.

News Editor
The Wall Street Journal

Random House New York

Library of Congress Cataloging-in-Publication Data

Malabre, Alfred L.
Beyond our means.

Includes index.
1. United States—Economic conditions—1945–
I. Title.
HC106.5.M24 1987   330.973'092   86-22002
ISBN 0-394-54345-9

MANUFACTURED IN THE UNITED STATES OF AMERICA
3 4 5 6 7 8 9

FOR BECKY, MAGGIE AND LIZZIE,
WHO NEVER WORRY ABOUT THESE THINGS

Contents

Introduction

In a play by the British playwright John Osborne entitled *Time, Present,* which packed the house in London's West End in the late 1960s, the heroine, Pamela, remarks at one point that "ever since I've been born there's been an economic crisis. . . . There's been no confidence . . . crashes, devaluing, loans and . . . at the end people are better off, better fed, better housed than ever, and if you never look at these forecasts, it makes no difference."

It's true. By virtually any standard of economic well-being, people are better off nowadays than when Pamela made these observations two decades ago. But this happy situation, I submit, can no longer prevail in the United States, and this book will explain why and suggest how the change will come about.

While I was preparing the final draft, my editor, Jason Epstein, asked me a question for which—as Jason surely knew—I had no ready answer. "How do I persuade the Random House sales staff," he asked, "that people will want to buy a book that's bad news? People always are willing to read about problems, but they also want solutions, the prospect of a happy ending."

One has only to scan the nonfiction best-seller lists to perceive the domination of how-to and can-do books. *The New York Times* has taken, in fact, to compiling a special best-seller list each week for how-to books. Titles there on a typical week in 1986 included *Fit for Life,* about a diet that promised to do just that for the book's readers; *Callanetics,* about exercises promising to make women look ten years youngers in only ten hours; and *The Be (Happy) Attitudes,* the upbeat advice of a California clergyman.

This book surely will never make that list. Its theme is stated in its title: *Beyond Our Means.* For a very long time, we've been living beyond our means—for so long, in fact, that now, sadly, it's beyond our means to put things right, at least in an orderly, reasonably painless manner.

It's tempting, of course, to recite all the awesome problems facing the American economy in the closing years of the twentieth century and then to apply the how-to, can-do approach; to paint a grim picture of the economic road ahead, for the nation as a whole and for individuals, that will draw in all the worriers—the people who buy how-to books by the bushel—and then explain that with a little effort things can be worked out nicely. It's tempting to suggest that all you have to do is write your congressman to do this or that, invest more money here and less there—and in the end your nest egg will survive, even grow. Your living standard will rise. As Pamela says, you will be better off, better fed, better housed than ever.

However much it may deter would-be readers, this book will lay out why the time for easy solutions to our accumulating economic difficulties has run out. No amount of governmental, or for that matter private, maneuvering will avert a very nasty time ahead. The bind is stated aptly by Jay W. Forrester, an economics professor at the Massachusetts Institute of Technology, when he says: "We are heading into difficult times and there isn't a great deal that can be done about it." Indeed, he adds, "such superficial issues as debates about the short-term business cycle or Republican versus Democratic political philosophy or shifts in tax policy can't significantly change the outlook."

If economic trouble lies inescapably ahead, what forms will it take? How did such a predicament arise in the first place? Where does the blame reside? As individuals, how best can we attempt to protect ourselves, to limit the damage, in the evolving situation?

If the answers supplied to such questions here provide scant comfort, so be it. If there's little in the end to give the Random House staff an upbeat message in the sales pitch, so be it. Perhaps, by looking at our predicament straight on, by assessing it as honestly as possible and attempting to understand its roots and its ramifications, we will better manage to cope. If that amounts to an exceedingly modest ambition, so be it.

In trying to provide some sort of an answer to Jason's question, I am reminded of my experiences in two great hurricanes—the awesome killer storm that raked the northeastern U.S. in September 1938 and the relatively recent hurricane named Gloria, which swept along a similar course almost exactly forty-seven years later. The 1938 hurricane was nameless, since it predated the practice of labeling hurricanes with names like Gloria or Ethel or Bob or Frank. It first struck land, sweeping up from the south across water, near Westhampton, New York, a resort town on Long Island's south shore, about eighty miles east of Manhattan. The winds reached well over a hundred miles an hour at the storm's peak, there was a tidal wave, and the clubhouse at the local golf course was brought into service as a morgue for those in the area who either drowned, were electrocuted by live wires, or were killed by collapsing walls or flying debris.

The winds in hurricane Gloria were nearly as intense as in the 1938 storm. Gloria, like the earlier hurricane, swept up from the south and crashed ashore on the south-facing beaches of Long Island. But there the similarities end. Gloria hit, mercifully, at dead low tide, while in 1938 the tide was at the full. Even more striking is the difference in preparations made prior to each storm. Before the 1938 hurricane, there was virtually no warning. Mrs. Kingman Brewster, whose husband was president of Yale for many years, recalled for me that as a young girl in Providence, Rhode Island, she saw scores of rats from the city's waterfront near her hilltop home a full day before the storm arrived. Somehow, the animals knew that a killer storm was on the way, even if humans didn't.

But there was no such warning in pancake-flat Westhampton. My first knowledge that something more than just a heavy storm was in progress occurred when a local policeman came to the door of our vacation cottage, which was just south of Westhampton's main street, perhaps a half mile from the beach. He told us to clear out fast and helped us hurry away, literally running for our lives. I can still recall his exact words: "Hurry up, the ocean is coming." And it was, right up our street, with its surging leading edge about a block to the south of us as we fled inland. Soon after we fled, our home was indeed inundated, and even the town's main street, inland of us, was under five feet of water at the hurricane's height.[1]

My first warning that Gloria might pose a problem for us came about a week before the storm at last arrived. The possibility that it might head our way was repeated and repeated on radio, television, and in all the newspapers, national as well as local. Public shelters were set up in the Westhampton area for storm refugees. I spent the preceding Thursday—Gloria struck around noon Friday—stocking up on such emergency supplies as flashlight batteries and a portable radio. Then I went about the house filling bathtubs to the brim with water that could serve for drinking and washing if my well, which operated on electricity, was put out of commission. Several hours before Gloria hit, a local policeman came to our door and urged us to move inland to a public shelter; I now live in Quogue, Westhampton's next-door neighbor to the east, in a house about the same distance from the beach as the one from which I had fled in 1938.

As things turned out, my decision to stay at home was correct. While I lost several trees, as well as all electrical power for about a week, my feet as well as my house kept dry.

Using my portable radio, I was able to follow Gloria's progress as the eye passed north across Long Island into New England, much as the 1938 storm had done. The evening after Gloria was gone, I enjoyed a candlelight dinner of cold cuts, cheese, and bread, washed down by a bottle of good wine supplied by my two refugee houseguests, Tom Royster and his wife, Linn, who had vacated their beachfront home the previous day after hearing all the warnings and who happily preferred my offer of hospitality to a night or two at the local shelter.

In the end, like the 1938 hurricane, Gloria proved to be a very costly affair, with its enormous wind damage. But the hardship that it caused would doubtless have been far more extensive had there been no warnings, as happened in 1938. And just as neither hurricane could have been prevented, it's my conviction that the next economic hurricane—the first to strike this nation since the Great Depression arrived in 1929—cannot be prevented. Its development is too far along. But if we are very fortunate, perhaps it will strike as Gloria did when the tide is low, when there are wise, quick-witted people in charge in Washington who will know how best to stem the economic damage. No matter when it does strike, we are surely better off forewarned, with our bathtubs full, fresh batteries in our flashlights, and our portable radios nearby.

To try to provide at least a sort of answer to Jason's question, this book is an early weather report on an economic hurricane that has been forming for a very long time and on the likely course it will take; as we shall see, there are several possibilities. Some estimates will be made as to just where it will strike and where the higher, safer ground may lie. But the main message here is that the hurricane can't be stopped, that we can only try to make things less nasty when it hits, and the first step in that modest effort is to understand the nature of the trouble.

A final footnote should be added about those two hurricanes. After they had passed and done their damage, the weather, which in each instance had been depressingly humid and enervating, turned cool and clear and remained that way for a long while.

BEYOND
OUR
MEANS

Chapter 1

On Borrowed Time

To start, a few statistics. Nine of every ten U.S. teenagers have their own camera. Seven of every ten own a stereo. One in three has a television set. One in five has a personal phone. One in six has an automobile. One in eight has a computer.

It may be comforting to suppose that the awesomely high living standard of most Americans—exemplified by this teenage affluence—is founded on unmatched know-how and industriousness. That, indeed, is the popular conception: a can-do nation, innovative and hard-working and therefore quite properly blessed with material benefits unrivaled in the world's less productive economies.

The truth is something else. The profusion of goods and services that most Americans enjoy in this century's closing years reflects a very different sort of tendency: to live beyond our means. Primarily this, and not some rare ability to deliver, underlies the seemingly boundless increase in American prosperity through much of the post-World War II era.

Debt is at the root of this tendency to live beyond our means. Massively, debt permeates our economy at all levels —personal, corporate, and governmental. The magnitudes are awesome. In all, as a nation, we are more than $7 trillion in debt—it's impossible to say the precise amount—and the total keeps soaring. It has nearly quadrupled since the mid-1970s. It now approximates $35,000 for each man, woman, and child in the nation. It comes to more than double the nation's yearly output of goods and services. The bulk of it— nearly half—is owed by businesses. The rest is owed, in nearly equal shares, by governmental units—mainly federal, but state and local as well—and by individuals. The federal portion alone recently swept past $2 trillion. Interest payments on this federal borrowing now exceed a tenth of all national income, twice the rate of a decade earlier.[1]

And while the pyramid of debt keeps mounting, the underlying collateral for the debt has begun to erode. Consumer borrowing is largely secured by housing, but the value of the nation's housing stock no longer rises apace; of late, home values in many areas have in fact been sinking. Plant and equipment, brick and mortar, underlie much of the debt that corporations owe, but at many corporations—a case in point is the steel business—such assets grow increasingly obsolete. As the recent proliferation of so-called junk bonds suggests, the quality of much corporate debt keeps deteriorating. Meanwhile, governmental debt rests largely on the tax base, yet the tax bite has narrowed in the wake of tax cutting and considerable corporate and individual tax breaks. From California to Massachusetts, voters have forced new limits on local tax authorities. The nation's vast infrastructure of roads, bridges, and other public facilities has been built largely through governmental borrowing. The burden of this debt keeps growing, but the infrastructure itself—witness the spread of potholes on many major roads—keeps deteriorating.

Our willingness, even determination, to live beyond our means—to go far more deeply into debt than our resources safely will allow—has led to other ominous patterns. As we have overborrowed, we have overspent. In late 1986, the share of after-tax income that Americans saved—including most money set aside for retirement—sank briefly below 2 percent. This was a postwar low, lower than the comparable reading for any other major industrial country and less than half the rate at which we saved only a decade ago.

We have tended as well to overpay ourselves. We complain—rarely blaming ourselves—that we are unable to compete with goods and services offered by our foreign competitors. Our balance of trade—our sales abroad minus what we purchase from foreigners—has swung in less than a decade from a multibillion-dollar surplus to a deficit far exceeding $100 billion a year.

This extravagance—our willingness to overpay ourselves with overvalued dollars and then to borrow and shop abroad, where things are cheaper—has led us finally to the unenviable status of debtor nation. In 1985, for the first time since early in the century, the U.S. owed more to the rest of the world than the rest of the world owed it. By late 1986, foreigners had over $1 trillion invested in the U.S., some $170 billion more than the total of U.S. investments abroad. The shortfall is expected to near $300 billion by 1988. As recently as 1982, American holdings abroad exceeded foreigners' assets in the U.S. by nearly $200 billion.

This new debtor status is precisely what has long prevailed —the condition has begun to assume a permanent look—in such financially troubled lands as Brazil, Mexico, and Argentina. Indebtedness has imposed no immediate adverse impact on the American economy. Indeed, foreigners' desire to hold American assets has helped the U.S. economy in a number of ways, from financing federal borrowing to suppressing U.S. inflation by tending to bolster the U.S. dollar. But if the trend persists, if America sinks deeper and deeper into debtor-nation status, painful bills will begin coming due. Americans will be compelled to give up more and more of their income simply to pay interest to overseas creditors. To service its global obligations, the U.S. will be forced to run larger and larger trade surpluses—there are none now—on goods and services, something that cannot be achieved without a severe further decline in the dollar's international value. We'll be forced, in other words, to sell our goods more cheaply, which means among other things paying ourselves less. Ultimately, the generous living standards that so many

Americans have enjoyed for so many years are bound to erode.

This book will document the long, dismal record of our post-World War II extravagance. It will show how, through a prosperity built on excessive debt, we have persistently, stubbornly lived far beyond our means—to a point where now, sadly, it is beyond our means to put things right readily. At long last we are facing an impasse, one of our own making. This book will explore our predicament, tracing its roots, and look ahead to the painful choices that now confront us.

ECONOMIC Cassandras have been issuing warnings for years. I know. As a financial writer, I've been bombarded with the gloomy press releases of such noted pessimists as Eliot Janeway and Howard Ruff for more years than I have gray hairs. But the dire consequences never seem to come to pass. Instead, employment and incomes rise, the two-car garage proliferates, roaming midwestern schoolteachers tour Paris and Rome, gourmet sections spring up and then swiftly expand in massive supermarkets as Americans consume seven hundred thousand pounds of caviar yearly, four times the late-1970s intake.

Notwithstanding all this, the scary scenarios keep arriving in the morning mail. A notable sample is contained in a 1985 issue of *International Moneyline,* an economic newsletter published by Julian M. Snyder. The issue outlines Snyder's "Armageddon" for the economy, an eventuality that he clearly regards as inescapable "sooner or later." The five-phase script begins with "stepped up money creation" in the face of "deflationary pressure and debt problems" and progresses through assorted economic difficulties until, with phase five, a depression settles in.

I continue, as I have done for more than a quarter century, to lob such hair-raising (and often headline-seeking) missives into a generous deskside wastebasket. But now I do so more gingerly and not without a quick glance and perhaps even a scribbled note or two for future reference—just in case. For as the nation's debt load—private as well as public—continues to pile up, as savings and investment keep lagging, as pay continues to outstrip comparable levels abroad while productivity remains lackluster, the dark pessimism of the apocalyptic forecasters grows less improbable.

Throughout our history we have shown an enviable disdain for limits, reflected in our national compulsion to consume and grow. We are not people accustomed to contraints—even as it becomes increasingly clear that we can no longer afford our aspirations. Meanwhile, the Reagan administration provides an extreme, even grotesque, illustration of our collective abandon in its reluctance to seek appreciably higher taxes or to rein in spending.

THE sources of today's predicament extend far back—beyond the last recession, beyond the long years of stagflation that marked much of the 1970s and late 1960s, even beyond the early post-World War II expansion, with its minimal inflation and unemployment levels. They reach all the way back to the grim, drab years of economic depression that preceded the Second World War, when unemployment wasn't 10 percent of the labor force or even 15 percent or 20 percent—but 25 percent. The combined losses of American corporations in some Great Depression years worked out to huge (for those times) numbers—$1.3 billion in 1932 and $1.2 billion in 1933.

Franklin Delano Roosevelt's New Deal was remedial and timely. The establishment of such agencies as the Federal Deposit Insurance Corporation (designed to safeguard savings with freshly printed dollar bills if need be) was and continues to be appropriate. But many of today's problems stem from the fact that Americans now feel entitled to the

hand-out programs these Despression-inspired measures
have become.

A statistic: Even after six years of Reagan, nearly one of
every two Americans depends entirely or in large part on
some variety of governmental "transfer" payment—money
gathered largely through taxation and then transferred to
individuals supposedly on the basis of need, but in reality,
more often than not largely unrelated to need. In the past
decade and a half, the number of Americans living largely or
entirely off a governmental check for which they perform no
labor has risen some 25 percent, to roughly 100 million. That
constitutes nearly one government-dependent individual for
each working citizen. In the early 1970s, this ratio was one in
three, one dependent for every three workers. The number
of government-dependent Americans approximates 150 million nowadays if one also includes people at work whose
employment depends on a government contract—such as a
worker building submarines for the Electric Boat division of
General Dynamics in Groton, Conn., for instance, or an economist at the University of Chicago who serves on the side as
consultant to the Commerce Department. The federal government now pays over $4,000 to each American each year
on the average, up from $1,705 in 1976 and only $685 in 1966.
The current total exceeds $7,000 if state and local govern-
ment payments are added.

Thirty-eight million Americans receive Social Security
payments, over 30 million get Medicare, some 23 million
receive Medicaid, over 20 million collect food stamps, chil-
dren from nearly 6 million households get school lunches,
and 2.8 million households receive public-housing benefits.
To this long list should be added more than 4 million recipients of Supplemental Security Income and some 11 million
recipients of so-called Aid to Families with Dependent Chil-
dren. To be sure, there is overlapping in these statistics, and
they do reflect many instances of bona fide need. But they
also reflect countless instances of "welfare" for the well off.

A twenty-year perspective, spanning the Johnson, Nixon, Ford, Carter, and early Reagan presidencies, shows the rise of transfer-payment entitlements in unmistakable terms. Over the twenty years, entitlement payments rose from 24 percent of federal spending to 41 percent. Some of this remarkable increase represents a noble determination to help the nation's needy with funds collected from relatively productive individuals. But the bulk of these huge payments clearly has been delivered to Americans who are relatively well off.[2] A 1986 study by the Heritage Foundation shows that one of every four recipients of low-cost Federal Housing Administration loans earns over $40,000 annually.

When welfare is called habit-forming, as it often is, the standard implication is that it's habit-forming for the indigent. But postwar experience in America shows that it's habit-forming for nearly everyone who receives it. In 1985, federal outlays for social programs reached an estimated $459 billion, a record, up from $307 billion in 1980, $166 billion in 1975, $73 billion in 1970, and $36 billion in 1965. Less than $100 billion of the latest total, however, represents money aimed mainly at helping the poor through such programs as Medicaid, public assistance, and food stamps. The bulk of the total, some $370 billion, comprises governmental nonpoverty payments for Social Security, Medicare, and federal employees' retirement. Through the past couple of decades, it should be added, by far the greatest spending growth has occurred within these nonpoverty categories. Just since 1980, such outlays have swelled about $130 billion, while antipoverty spending has risen only some $20 billion.

THE corporate scene is similar. In 1984 alone, the government paid $14 billion in direct support for programs designed to assist American businesses in such diverse areas as energy and aeronautical research, farm-price maintenance, shipbuilding, and mineral exploration. In addition, corporations

benefited to the tune of some $68 billion through tax breaks
ranging from investment-tax credits to the exclusion of interest payments on so-called industrial development bonds issued through state and local governments.

In a recent four-year period, General Dynamics earned
nearly $2 billion but, by taking advantage of various corpo-
rate tax breaks, paid no federal income taxes. Other business
giants that paid not a nickel in federal income taxes in the
same period include DuPont, which had profits of nearly $4
billion, General Mills, which earned over $1 billion, and W.
R. Grace & Co., with a net of $483 million. In all, forty major
companies paid no federal taxes in the four years and many
claimed tax *refunds* from the government totaling hundreds
of millions.

THE largest income-transfer program is Social Security,
which distributed approximately $185 billion in 1985, some
$70 billion more than five years earlier. And projections show
that the yearly totals will reach about a quarter of a trillion
dollars by the end of this decade, a trend that results from a
declining ratio of tax-paying workers to check-collecting re-
tirees, along with cost-of-living adjustments in monthly payments that have perennially overcompensated for inflation.[3]

The popular conception, or misconception, is that the nation's elderly as a rule suffer much deprivation. Yet the over-
sixty-five-year-old population enjoys a per capita yearly
income that's actually higher—by $335 in 1985—than that of
the citizenry as a whole. And if benefits are taken into account, the percentage of elderly poor—at 3.3 percent—is far
lower than among the nation generally. Moreover, a survey
of new Social Security recipients by the General Accounting
Office in Washington shows that 91.3 percent have such additional sources of income as public and private pension programs (68 percent), earned income (49 percent), and income
from stocks, bonds, and other such assets (67 percent).

It is nonsense to assert that Social Security payments are merely sums that have been paid into the program by the recipients. Consider, for instance, a worker who began paying into the system in 1937, when it was launched, and worked until 1982. If he had paid the maximum in Social Security taxes each of the forty-five working years, his payments would have totaled $12,828. His benefits would have begun at $734 a month. If he were married, his wife would collect half of his benefit, or an additional $367 monthly, bringing their total first-year benefit to $13,217, or more than he had paid in the forty-five years of employment.

At age sixty-five, moreover, he had a life expectancy of 14.2 more years and his wife had a life expectancy of 18.5 more years. This means that if Social Security benefits were to keep increasing at the same rate at which they rose in the fourteen years prior to his retirement, the combined benefits for the retiree and his wife would come to $2,632 a month at the time of his death. Then his widow would become eligible to collect an indexed pension of $1,316 monthly. Thus, the couple's lifetime Social Security benefits, based on average life expectancies, would amount to some $375,000—all from a contribution of $12,828.[4]

The Commerce Department reckons that an over-sixty-five couple needs appreciably less in income to live at a given standard than a similar couple younger than sixty-five. After taking into account the tax status of Social Security income and special tax benefits for the elderly, Commerce officials estimate that an individual with a preretirement income of $10,000 annually would require only about $8,180 in income after retiring to maintain the same living standard. A person earning $25,000 before retirement would need only about $18,000.

In our concern for the elderly, we have equated them with the poor. However, it's clear that as a group they are relatively well off—better off, in fact, than most younger citizens. In the late 1960s, about one quarter of aged Americans lived below the government-defined poverty level—twice the poverty rate for the U.S. population as a whole. Now, the poverty rate for elderly Americans is down to about 12 percent, which is actually two percentage points lower than the overall poverty rate. Meanwhile, about 10 percent of Social Security spending goes to households with independent incomes of more than $30,000. We have created a system of transfer payments that shifts funds not from the rich to the poor, but mainly from the young to the old.

RECIPIENTS of military pensions are among the wealthiest 20 percent of all U.S. households. And some 60 percent of all military retirement benefits—an estimated $18.3 billion was paid out in 1986—goes to such households. The median age of a new military pensioner is only forty-one; two thirds of all military retirees still work and only 15 percent are over sixty-five. Under generous rules, individuals can retire after twenty years of service and receive 50 percent of their base pay. Such pensions now account for some 8 percent of all military expenditures, up from less than 2 percent in the early 1960s.[5]

In 1985, according to the Department of Education, over 13,000 students in families earning more than $100,000 yearly were receiving low-interest government loans for college. (A Harris poll shows that 77 percent of Americans feel that too many well-to-do youths receive such loans.) Among 106 New York City area residents sued by the government in 1985 for defaulting on such loans after college, five were budding investment bankers, five were doctors, two were dentists, and others included college professors, accountants, computer programmers, and even three policemen.[6] I am reminded of a young friend of mine, an upstanding youth from a family whose yearly income approached $200,000 a year. While at Yale in the late 1970s, when the loan program was even more generous than in later years and there were no income limits on applicants, my friend borrowed some $7,000. His Yale education fully paid for by his parents, he then turned around and invested the loan money in a certificate of deposit yielding some 14 percent, or roughly double the amount he would owe in interest on the government-subsidized loan. His attitude was that if the government was silly enough to allow him to pick up some $500 a year quite legally and quite without effort, why not do it? He told me at the time, I should add, that his maneuver was by no means unique on campus. He said that most of his Yale pals, similarly well heeled, were doing the same thing.

The picture is much the same on the farm. A 1986 study by the General Accounting Office (GAO) in Washington shows that two thirds of direct federal farm subsidies go to farmers who are relatively well off, with little debt and few financial worries. The reason, according to the GAO, is that the subsidies are based largely on production and so wind up mostly in the hands of the bigger, richer farm operators.

In 1984, for instance, the government paid out $3.3 billion in direct farm subsidies, and $2.1 billion of this went to farmers with debt-to-assets ratios of less than 40 percent, a relatively sound level. These farmers, in fact, are defined by the Department of Agriculture as having "few financial problems and very strong net worth." Another $753 million of the $3.3 billion went to farmers with debt-to-assets ratios between 40 percent and 69 percent. And a mere $400 million went to farmers with debt ratios of 70 percent or more. This latter level is deemed dangerously high by the department's analysts.

THE rise of transfer payments since the early years of the Great Depression has been remarkable. In 1929 and again in 1930, transfer payments totaled $1.5 billion. As the slump worsened, the sums transferred yearly moved slowly up into the $2 billion-plus area. But as the Depression dragged on, the yearly transfers showed only modest gains. In some years, in fact, the totals dropped—as in 1932, to $2.2 billion from $2.7 billion in 1931, and as in 1937, to $2.4 billion from $3.5 billion in 1936. As late as 1940, the total transferred was $3.1 billion, only slightly higher than the $2.7 billion paid out in 1931, before the New Deal programs were even in place. At $3.5 billion in 1936, transfer payments actually fell through the second half of the depressed 1930s.

All through this period, of course, new income-transfer arrangements were being established under Roosevelt's leadership. For example, a single day during the so-called Hundred Days of the new president's first term—May 12, 1933—witnessed three pieces of legislation that would eventually boost transfer payments mightily. These were the Federal Emergency Relief Act, which funneled some $5 billion in direct relief money to states, cities, towns, and counties; the Agricultural Adjustment Act, which provided several hundred million dollars to farmers for not planting crops and channeled large amounts of food free to relief families; and the Emergency Farm Mortgage Act, which halted foreclosures and provided federal refunding of mortgages.

After the war, transfer payments soared. An economist visiting from Mars, if asked to inspect the record of transfer payments for a clue to when times were really bad in America, would surely conclude that by comparison with the 1930s, the postwar decades were years of deep depression, for after the relatively flat showing of the 1930s, transfer payments began to escalate steeply. From $1.5 billion in 1930, $3.1 billion in 1940, and $3.6 billion in 1944, the last full year of the war, the yearly totals moved sharply higher. They rose to $6.2 billion in 1945 and $11.3 billion in 1946. By 1950, the total was up to $15.1 billion; by 1960, to $28.5 billion; by 1970, to $79.9 billion; and by the start of the present decade, to $297.6 billion. For all the Reagan team's rhetoric about spending restraint, the $500-billion mark is fast approaching. For perspective, it's noteworthy that transfer payments have climbed roughly three hundredfold since the Depression, while the consumer price index has risen only about seven-fold.

In 1930, transfer payments comprised 1.9 percent of all personal income. By 1940, the rate reached 4 percent. By 1950, it was 6.6 percent; by 1960, 7.1 percent; by 1970, 10 percent; by 1980, 13.7 percent. Recently, the rate has approximated 15 percent.

The message is plain enough. Programs instituted decades ago to keep the economy together in a very bad time have become a permanent and increasingly influential feature of the prosperous postwar era. To be sure, the transfer-payment numbers encompass a very wide assortment of programs—from sundry Social Security benefits to pensions for the military to all manner of welfare. Nonetheless, a huge slice of the swiftly mounting sums transferred each postwar year reflects long-ago legislation aimed initially, and quite properly, at fighting the Great Depression. Now, as we have seen, the bulk of the money winds up not with the needy but within the prosperous American mainstream.

SINCE the late 1970s, I have periodically consulted several economists to ascertain whether they felt that another Great Depression might be just over the horizon. These include several Nobel laureates, former Federal Reserve Board chairmen and the like, such people as Paul Samuelson, Milton Friedman, Arthur Burns, and John Kenneth Galbraith. By and large, they have consistently discounted the likelihood of another Great Depression. And time and again, a major factor in this optimism has been transfer payments, the conviction that the huge rise in such income through the postwar years precludes the sort of collapse that occurred in the 1930s. The various economists maintain steadfastly that the rise in transfers, especially to jobless individuals during recessionary stages of the business cycle, has meant that the demand for goods and services will not again shrink—as happened in the Great Depression—no matter how much unemployment spreads.

There's no doubt that the rising flow of income transfers, by and large from producers to nonproducers, has fed the postwar prosperity and limited the severity of the various postwar recessions. It has served as a built-in stabilizer—to borrow the economic jargon—against any self-feeding cyclical contraction of economic activity. It has, without a doubt, kept the money flowing in times of spreading joblessness, when otherwise there would surely have been a nasty shortage of demand. Always, in contrast to the Depression years, Americans collectively have had the income, be it earned or transferred, to maintain demand for goods and services until a recovery comes around once again.

But with the rise in transfers has come the rise in federal debt. Moreover, this income-stabilizing process has produced a change in attitudes. We now expect that Uncle Sam will somehow always provide our financial support.

Those of us whose memories stretch back beyond the relatively prosperous postwar era to the Great Depression may sense additional changes. No one in the couple of decades that spanned the Depression, World War II, and the early postwar era applied the term *workaholic* to a man like my father, a busy family doctor. The connotation nowadays is slightly unpleasant, suggesting excessive, perhaps even pointless, labor, as if one were addicted to a potentially destructive substance. But in my father's time his daily routine, which stretched from 7 A.M. to late evening and included many house calls between long office hours and hospital duty, was simply the typical schedule of a hard-working man. There was nothing distasteful about it.

Another sign of change comes to mind. I have lived in Manhattan most of my life and for nearly three decades have motored on Friday afternoons to a summer cottage some eighty-five miles to the east in a tiny Long Island village called Quogue. When this Friday routine began, in the early 1960s, I found that by escaping my office no later than 4:30 P.M. I was able to exit the city slightly ahead of a rush-hour-plus-end-of-the-week exodus, a maneuver that chopped perhaps a half hour from the eastward drive. By the early 1970s, however, I discovered that to maintain my slight lead on the rush-hour surge, I had to slip out of the office by no later than 4 P.M. And in recent years, the getaway hour has moved even earlier: Now I have to be on the road by 3 P.M. or be prepared for stop-go, stop-go. Meanwhile, I've found that the trip east, in sharp contrast to a couple of decades ago, has become relatively traffic free at what was once the rush hour, 5 to 6 P.M. By that late in the day, the bulk of Friday's eastbound early-leavers have already flown the office coop.

SUCH developments may partly reflect a rising living standard for people who can leave their office earlier on account of high productivity—and not simply a rising aversion to hours on the job. Whatever the explanation, a 1984 survey found that about half of the nation's citizens were largely satisfied with their situation. That was precisely double the comparable percentage in a similar poll taken five years earlier. Moreover, as many as 70 percent of those interviewed believed that an individual could begin life poor in America and end it rich, through hard work and perhaps a modicum of good fortune.[7]

Other statistics support this optimism. Since 1970, per capita income in the U.S. has risen, after eliminating gains reflecting rising prices, by about one third. Roughly one person in eight now lives below a so-called poverty line, which itself is constantly being moved upward by the Washington bureaucracy. A generation ago, the comparable ratio was one in five. The number of black Americans in college nowadays is four times higher than a quarter century ago. In about a decade, the economy has spawned—notwithstanding repeated recessions—some 20 million additional jobs. Even Jerry Rubin, the former radical, migrated to Wall Street. And for all the talk of lawlessness, the crime rate has been dropping. In a recent twelve months, the number of U.S. households touched by criminal activity fell 29 percent, the largest such drop in a nearly a decade.

On the other hand, American productivity—our ability to turn out goods and services of a high quality and with reasonable efficiency—is lagging further and further behind that of other key industrial countries. In recent decades, moreover, productivity gains have been narrowing. In the 1960s, workers' hourly output rose at an average annual rate of 2.44 percent. But in the 1970s, this dropped to 1.14 percent yearly, and roughly that reduced rate of gain has persisted through much of the 1980s. By no coincidence, the buying power of the average paycheck—a yardstick that many economists use to gauge living standards—has tended to increase more slowly. In the long run, living standards depend on productivity; we can live on borrowed money for the time being, but ultimately we can't spend more than we produce.[8]

A 1984 study by A. B. Laffer Associates, a Los Angeles-based economics consultant, shows how transfer payments can diminish the work incentive among able-bodied people. It assesses the effect of taxes and wages on disposable income, including transfer-payment income, for a Los Angeles-area family of four. As wages rise—and welfare payments decline accordingly—spendable income actually shrinks at several stages along the way. When this typical family of four's monthly wage level moves up from $600 to $700, its spendable income actually drops $5, as a result of higher taxes and reduced transfer payments. At $800 a month, family income declines another $5. The Laffer study shows that tiny income gains do occur as the wage level continues up to $900 monthly and then $1,000. But at $1,100, spendable income drops by $178, and at $1,200 it declines by another $39. Persistent gains in spendable income don't occur until monthly wages are safely above $1,300.

Along the same line is a hypothetical illustration contained in *Losing Ground,* a recent book by Charles Murray of the Manhattan Institute for Policy Research. Murray sets up the case of a mythical couple, Harold and Phyllis, who reside in Pennsylvania. It is 1960 and she is pregnant, a circumstance that, according to Murray, mandates their marrying and avoiding going on welfare—at least in 1960, when child-rearing benefits were relatively slim and would be cut dollar for dollar if Phyllis assumed a part-time job. Harold, meanwhile, wouldn't be allowed to reside with Phyllis for as long as the family received these benefits.

Typically, therefore, Harold takes a low-skilled job in order to support his new family; he hopes, with hard work and a bit of good fortune, to move slowly up the employment ladder.

Murray further explains how the decision for Harold and Phyllis would probably change by 1970. By then, he notes, child-rearing benefits are sharply higher, and President Johnson's Great Society initiatives have created various additional welfare programs—Medicaid, food stamps, and housing subsidies, to name a few. New rules now permit Phyllis to work part-time and retain the first $30 that she earns; above that, her child-care benefits are cut by $2 for every additional $3 earned. At the same time, on account of a 1968 Supreme Court ruling, Harold is now allowed to stay in the house without losing the family's benefits and, so long as he isn't responsible under law for the child, his income won't count against the child-care payments.

In the circumstances prevailing in 1970, Murray observes, Harold can marry Phyllis and work forty hours a week in a tough, tiring job or he can live with Phyllis and their baby "without getting married, not work and have more disposable income." The likely decision isn't difficult to guess.

AFTER World War II, economists worried that without military demand, business activity would fall steeply. They feared another depression, but in fact nothing like a depression happened. Though a bona fide recession was in fact recorded by the National Bureau of Economic Research, the nonprofit organization that serves as official arbiter in such matters, it lasted only eight months, from February 1945 to October 1945. Soon the economy entered three years of sustained expansion. Even with the massive shift from military to civilian jobs, unemployment edged down. By late 1948—by which time, it had been feared, a deep new slump would be under way—the economy was in fact setting new records of prosperity.

What went right? Why were the gloomy forecasts so wrong? Where had the business prophets miscalculated?

To understand where the pessimists erred, let's look at some statistics of the amount of after-tax income that Americans were saving. In 1938, the saving rate was only 1.1 percent, but higher than what had prevailed earlier in the 1930s, when the Depression was at its worst. In 1934, the saving rate was only 0.7 percent. In 1932 and again in 1933, it was actually negative, when consumption plus tax payments in those dreadful years exceeded income; this was possible because so many people were using past savings, as well as debt, in order to shelter, clothe, and feed themselves.

With the advent of the war, however, a remarkable change began to occur in the savings pattern. In 1939, with Europe at war and concern rising that the U.S. might soon also be involved, the saving rate edged up to 3.7 percent. In 1940, it hit 5.1 percent. And then, as the U.S. finally became directly involved, the rate started soaring—to 11.8 percent in 1941, to 23.6 percent in 1942, to 25 percent in 1943, to a record 25.5

percent in 1944, the last complete year of hostilities. In 1945, the rate began to move down again. At 19.7 percent of after-tax income, however, it remained unusually high, dwarfing most earlier readings.[9]

In retrospect, there's nothing mysterious about the sharp buildup of savings during the war. In absolute terms, the sums saved each year swelled from less than $1 billion in 1938 to a wartime high of nearly $40 billion in 1944, a direct consequence of wartime austerity. People were enjoying large increases in their earnings, and a much higher percentage of the working-age population had jobs. There was a rush from the campus to the barracks, and women who only a few years before hadn't the remotest thought of entering the labor market found themselves holding down high-paying jobs in offices and factories supplying the war effort. Between 1941, when the U.S. entered the war, and 1944, even with the movement of civilian jobholders into the military, there was a 3.6 million increase in the number of civilian employees. Over the preceding decade, by comparison, there was a 2 million decline. But there was little available in the way of goods and services on which this swelling work force could spend its pay during the war years. While pay was sharply on the rise—having more than doubled, from $52.1 billion in 1940 to $123.1 billion in 1945—consumption lagged far behind. Consumer outlays for so-called durable goods—automobiles especially—fell by one third between 1941 and 1944. Even spending for services, ranging from shelter to schooling, rose only slightly. The pattern was much the same for so-called nondurable commodities such as gasoline, which of course was strictly rationed in the war years.

This combination of sharply rising pay and limited spending opportunities resulted in the massive buildup in savings in those years. Peace brought a steep increase in the public's demand for all sorts of goods and services. The government didn't begin to compile broad inventory statistics until a few years later, so it's impossible to pinpoint precisely how bare the cupboard was when the war ended. It's clear, though, that factories were hard pressed for many months to meet the abrupt surge in demand for civilian items. Consumers were flush as never before, and it became increasingly evident that they intended to go out and spend much of their bulging savings.

Analysts who anticipated a return to the slump of the 1930s failed to appreciate the crucial role that these savings would play in postwar prosperity. And those who were aware of the statistics seemed to assume that much of the money would merely stagnate in bank vaults, earning only modest interest, instead of being spent.

POSTWAR prosperity had many causes, but none seems more important than the willingness, even eagerness, of Americans to spend what they had been forced to save during the war. The trend of savings was nearly as remarkable in those early postwar years as it had been in wartime. Where the saving rate soared in wartime, it began to shrivel in peacetime.

From 19.7 percent in 1945, the saving rate plummeted to 9.5 percent in 1946, followed by further, less precipitous declines. By the early 1950s, the rate settled into a range of from 8 percent to as low as 6 percent. Meanwhile, consumption rose sharply. At $109.1 billion in 1944, personal outlays moved up to $120.7 billion in 1945. Then, with the arrival of peace, consumer buying gained still more momentum. Expenditures rose to $144.8 billion in 1946, to $179.2 billion by the end of the decade and, with uninterrupted increases even through the Korean War, to the area of $260 billion by the mid-1950s.

In a decade, consumer spending multiplied two and a half times. And because inflation remained relatively low through much of the early postwar period, the year-to-year increases were largely "real," not distorted by price changes.

Incomes rose briskly in those years, but at nothing like the pace of spending. The gains in income, taken alone, hardly suggest the sort of spending surge that erupted. The surge becomes readily plausible, however, if the steep decline in the saving rate is taken into account as well.

WHY was the public so willing to consume its savings so soon after the Great Depression? The late John Maynard Keynes had feared that reluctance of people to consume would result, without government action, in periodic "liquidity traps" where spending, and ultimately general economic activity, would stagnate. What concerned him in the 1930s was that unless people spent more, the Depression might be endless.

In the early postwar years, analysts who feared such a liquidity trap were wrong partly because they ignored the role of transfer payments, which had originated during the 1930s. In the early postwar years, these payments still were a relatively minor part of the overall economic picture, but they seemed nonetheless to have convinced Americans that the government would see to their needs whether they saved or not. In fact, transfer payments should have received very careful scrutiny from business forecasters, for as the various benefit programs became more and more generous, the need and therefore the impulse to save for a rainy day diminished.

It's noteworthy that in countries whose governments provide relatively skimpy retirement benefits, rates of income saved each year tend to be remarkably high. In Japan, whose governmental retirement program isn't as generous as Social Security in the U.S., the saving rate has exceeded 20 percent-through much of the postwar period. And the propensity of the Japanese to save runs a good deal deeper than simply an awareness that retirement lies ahead. Ten Americans interviewed in New Jersey in 1985 by *The Wall Street Journal* were willing to take risks by going deeply into debt. As one put it, only in America can you buy a house when the husband and wife are unemployed. But eight Japanese in Tokyo also interviewed expressed great reluctance about running down their savings and overborrowing. Only two of the eight used credit cards. One, who earned only $14,000, still managed to save $2,700 a year, nearly 20 percent of his pay. He lived with his parents and paid them $120 monthly for room and board and used $400 a month for pocket money.

When the American economy emerged from the war, there were a number of strong and unusual incentives, legislated years earlier, that spurred Americans to spend rather than save. Among the most powerful of these was a provision allowing homeowners to deduct mortgage-interest payments from their income for tax purposes, deductions which most major countries did not allow. There can be little question that the mortgage-interest deduction—which remains in the latest tax law—not only helped fuel the postwar housing boom but turned many potential savers into spenders.

Tax regulations encouraged other sorts of spending as well. In the U.S., in contrast to many other countries, the interest expense of anything bought on credit—cars, refrigerators, furniture, power boats—could, until the latest law, be charged against income. Thus, borrowing often made far more sense than saving, and so the spending binge continued.

Furthermore, postwar inflation has tended to erode savings in many countries, but in the U.S. the saving rate was already exceptionally low when the price spiral became severe. The saving rate was 8.1 percent of income in the late 1960s, before inflation began to accelerate. For another half decade, the saving rate remained at about 8 percent, even with persistently severe inflation. Eventually, however, as the perception spread that a new inflationary climate had set in, the already feeble propensity to save waned. The saving rate edged down progressively, reaching 4.8 percent in the early 1980s. Even in absolute terms, the amount of money being saved each year diminished. It fell some $20 billion in the early 1980s, in the wake of the 1979–80 price explosion. In real terms, of course, the decline was still sharper because dollars saved in, say, 1983 were worth far less than those put away in 1981. In brief, as inflation worsened through the latter postwar years, it paid to spend rather than save.

OUR declining ability to keep up with international competition in recent years seems due in part to our dismal level of personal savings. Savings, after all, provide capital for industrial growth and modernization, which in turn enhance productivity. Ultimately, much of the blame rests with a U.S. tax system that has spurred borrowing through overly generous deductions and then has discouraged saving by taxing it twice—once when the money is earned and again when it produces income in a savings account or other interest-bearing or dividend-yielding investment.

In 1985, capital outlays in the U.S. amounted to an estimated 18 percent of the country's gross national product. The comparable investment rates were 30 percent in Japan, 22 percent in West Germany, 20 percent in France, and 19 percent in both Italy and Canada. Among the major nations, only Britain, with a rate of 17 percent, was below the U.S. level.

The result is that a disturbingly large portion of America's plant and equipment has grown obsolete. The most glaring situation, perhaps, is in the so-called smokestack region near the Great Lakes, where such industries as steel have fallen further and further behind their overseas rivals in their efforts to install modern, efficient machinery. It's no coincidence that Japan's saving rate is up in the 20 percent area and that Japan's production facilities are generally much more efficient than comparable facilities in the U.S.

In the very long run, the tendency to spend too much and save too little hobbles economic growth. Without increas-

ingly efficient facilities, productivity advances become
harder and harder to achieve. And without advancing productivity, living standards stop rising and eventually fall.
Even in the shorter term, a low savings level can limit the
economy's growth. If savings had been low as World War II
ended, instead of sky-high, it's a safe bet that the postwar
surge in business activity never would have occurred, and
those who anticipated a deep, early postwar slump would
probably have been right.

The paucity of savings now poses a problem for policy-
makers that defies a simple, painless solution. As a democracy
we have made a choice, unfortunately a short-sighted one.
We spend freely, and accordingly, many of us live very well
indeed. Our choice has been facilitated by regulations that
our elected officials have formulated with our ballot-box ap-
proval. It's all in keeping with a national character that gives
frugality short shrift and imagines that economic limits make
little sense.

Chapter 2

Borrow and Buy

While the saving rate has dwindled since World War II, the rate of borrowing has risen sharply. In early 1947, consumer installment loans amounted to just over 2 percent of personal income. Within two years, it rose to 5 percent. By the late 1950s, the rate moved above 10 percent and continued to climb through the 1960s and 1970s. By 1979, the rate exceeded 15 percent, and in the 1980s, after a dip in the recession-plagued early 1980s, the upward trend has continued. Recently, it has neared 20 percent.

Other indexes of borrowing show a similar pattern through the postwar years. In absolute terms, the volume of consumer-installment debt outstanding in 1985, approximating $500 billion, was roughly thirty times higher than in 1950. Noninstallment debt—mainly, credit scheduled to be repaid in lump sums—has also soared, to about $100 billion, more than ten times its 1950 level. These spectacular gains don't take into account an enormous rise in mortgage borrowing, which at nearly $2 trillion has, like installment debt, swelled to about thirty times its 1950 level. The vast bulk of this debt is owed by owners of one-to-four family houses and apartment dwellers.

Such precipitous increases would perhaps be of minor concern were it clear that servicing the debt load posed no particular problem. But that, unfortunately, isn't the situation. Rising indebtedness may pose little difficulty if the underlying collateral supporting the debt expands apace. However, as we've seen in the previous chapter, this is hardly the case. And so the borrowing grows ever more fragile, a pattern that worsens as the the postwar years roll on.

By the mid-1950s, the number of consumer-installment loans delinquent thirty days or more amounted to less than 1.5 percent of the total outstanding. Even in the periodic recessions that struck in the early 1960s and again in the early 1970s, the loan delinquency rate remained safely below 2 percent. But in the more recent recessions of the mid-1970s and early 1980s, such delinquencies reached the area of 3 percent, more than twice the mid-1950s rate. In recent years, moreover, the delinquency rate has held appreciably above the 2 percent mark even in prosperous times, with no recession in sight. In early postwar years, this barometer of the public's ability to service debt often remained under 2 percent even during slumps.

Still more troubling is the behavior of a similar measure that monitors debt-servicing difficulties among people who have taken out home-mortgage loans. In 1985, some 6 percent of home-mortgage loans were in arrears thirty days or longer. That's up from 3 percent in the early 1970s and only 2 percent in the late 1950s. Even with a reviving economy after the 1981–82 recession, the rate continued rising. In late 1984, a year of brisk business growth, a record 550,000 home mortgages were at least thirty days past due, and some 63,000 homes were facing foreclosure.

Such percentages may seem small. However, the postwar trend toward higher and higher rates of delinquency is troubling, for these are uncharted waters. Reliable debt-servicing data simply didn't exist in the years before the Second World War, so no one knows just where the point of danger may lie. It's encouraging that there has been no marked increase in the rates at which items bought on credit are being repossessed by lending institutions. At less than 1 percent, the repossession rate on automobiles was no higher in 1984 than in the mid-1970s. The mobile-home repossession rate has remained under 1.5 percent for a decade, after briefly broaching the 2 percent level in 1973–74, an increase that had more to do with the oil embargo and steep oil-price increase by the cartel of oil-exporting nations than with overburdened borrowers.

A continuing low level of repossessions, however, is no guarantee against an abrupt increase in repayment difficulties in the future, particularly in any new economic slump. So long as the postwar erosion of savings persists, along with high rates of borrowing, the danger increases that consumers on a broad scale will at some point find themselves unable to service their loans.

But where is that danger point? Is it when installment-loan delinquencies reach 3.5 percent or 4 percent or 4.5 percent or even 5 percent? Is it when mortgage delinquencies top 9 percent or 10 percent or higher still? No one knows, but it is clear that consumers are assuming more and more debt and encountering more and more difficulty servicing it.[1]

This pattern would be less worrisome if it were apparent that planners in Washington and in corporate boardrooms knew how to guide the economy along a recession-free path of year-in and year-out expansion. However, as we will see, they don't. Economic slumps, like death and taxes, remain an inescapable part of our future.

A few statistics help to underline the rise of consumer indebtedness in recent years. From 1974 to 1984, for example, overall consumer debt rose 173 percent, and debt per person soared from $10,264 to $26,566. The rise is smaller, of course, if inflation is taken into account. But it still amounts to about 30 percent.

As steep as these increases are, they are milder than corresponding increases in corporate and governmental indebtedness over the same span. The amount of business debt outstanding rose 188 percent in the same ten years. Sharper still was the rise in debt owed by federal, state, and local governments, which was up 190 percent.

A measure of business debt is the so-called quick ratio—the ratio of corporate cash plus such assets as Treasury bills to corporate debt obligations due within a year or less. It has shrunk, with occasional interruptions, over the postwar decades, suggesting that corporations are increasingly strapped for funds.

In the late 1940s, the quick ratio for manufacturing firms, for example, was 1.07. In other words, the cash and cashlike assets of these corporations slightly exceeded their liabilities due within a year. By the late 1950s, this ratio was down to 0.57, a decline of nearly one half. Within another decade, it was at only 0.23. And by the early 1980s, it was at about 0.15, a small fraction of its early postwar levels. The lower the ratio, the more likely it is that a company may have difficulty paying its bills.

Another such barometer of corporate debt is the ratio of short-term corporate debt to overall corporate debt, including long-term borrowing. A company with a relatively low short-term debt ratio tends to be under less debt-servicing strain than one whose ratio is on the high side, for short-term debt obviously represents a more pressing obligation than long-term debt. As recently as 1969, this ratio was less than .23. By the early 1970s, it crossed above .30, and it has continued climbing erratically since then. By the early 1980s, it was at .35.

As with consumer debt, it's unclear just when corporate debt becomes dangerously excessive. How low, for example, must the quick ratio fall before corporations generally are unable to service their borrowing? How high must the short-term debt ratio move before there's a widespread failure to pay liabilities coming due?

The danger point may be even closer for corporations than

for consumers and homeowners. Perhaps the clearest indication is the pattern of business failures, which have risen explosively, far outstripping the dollar's depreciation. This can be seen in a series compiled by Dun & Bradstreet, Inc., that tracks current liabilities—bills due within a year or less—of business enterprises that fail each month. In the late 1940s, liabilities were running at roughly $200 million a year. By the mid-1950s, the total crossed $400 million. By 1961, the $1 billion level was reached, and a decade later the $2 billion mark. Since then, the already steep rise has accelerated. The liabilities figure reached $4.4 billion in 1975, edged down for several years, and then soared by 1982, a recession year, to nearly $9 billion, an increase of more than fourfold in a decade. In a single month in that year, the failure figure matched the total for the entire postwar era up to 1956, a span encompassing two recessions.

After years of borrowing excessively, businesses are strapped to a point where the failure level now routinely sends shudders across the entire economic landscape. With each new recession, the situation grows more ominous. For all their borrowing and skimpy savings, consumers' behavior seems downright frugal compared to what has been happening at the corporate level. Junk bonds, for example, are a boardroom concept and not something concocted at consumer level.

The increasing use of so-called junk bonds in corporate takeover situations is perhaps the most flagrant illustration of the debt buildup within corporations. As recently as a decade ago, some $1 billion of such lowly rated bonds were issued, but now the total exceeds $15 billion. This surge has been in securities whose quality is deemed so shaky by the various credit-rating services that they appear suitable vehicles for only the most daring investors, intent on extra-high rates of interest. Early on, these junk securities were issued mainly by unproven growth companies or troubled industrial giants,

such as Chrysler Corp., desperate for capital and willing to
pay inordinately high interest rates.

More recently, however, junk bonds have been issued
mainly by shell corporations, enterprises devoid of valuable
assets, in order to finance highly leveraged acquisitions of
other, often larger and healthier, corporations. This, clearly,
is a very new situation. More than 80 percent of these bonds
have never endured the test of general economic downturn
or a sustained period of rising interest rates. As Pete V.
Domenici, the Republican senator from New Mexico who
chaired the Senate Budget Committee, has noted, "Comparing today's explosion of junk bonds with their use in the late
1970s is like comparing World War II with the Civil War
simply because gunpowder was used in both."

Further spurring the debt buildup is a recent tactic of
lenders called securitization, whereby loan-backed securities, such as shares of common stock, are sold to the public.
A typical issue might be backed, for example, by automobile
loans that are coming due. In essence, securitization has
opened the way for the creation of marketable securities to
finance loans traditionally made by banks, finance companies, retailers, and other lenders. Securitization offers so
many advantages to lenders that it's likely to grow rapidly—
perhaps to $20 billion in 1986 and still more sharply there-
after. With the advent of securitization, it's also clear that
debt, already so pervasive in our economy, will spread further. Moreover, if the borrowers in a particular securitization
deal should fail to meet their commitments, the shareholders
of the securities, and not the bank or finance company, will
be left in the lurch. In short, the spread of securitization
suggests that if extensive debt-servicing problems crop up in
the years just ahead, the impact will be even broader than
might otherwise have been the case.

Recently, corporate debt amounted to over 81 percent of
so-called book value—the value of a company according to its
accounting records, normally computed by subtracting all

debts from assets. This was up from an estimated 68 percent at the start of this decade. And using actual market value— the combined worth of company stock on equity exchanges —the debt-to-value ratio has recently approximated 100 percent.

EVEN corporate borrowing, however, can't match what the federal government has done. Federal debt has nearly tripled within a decade. To be sure, there are important distinctions. Consumers and private businesses, as well as state and local governmental units, can't create money as the federal government can through so-called open market operations of the Federal Reserve System. In such operations, the Federal Reserve trades Treasury bills and similar issues in ways designed to regulate the growth of the nation's money supply.

The money supply tends to expand when the Fed buys securities from private dealers and to diminish when the Fed sells to dealers. When it buys from dealers, it pays by crediting the various dealer accounts, thus pumping money into the private economy. This, in brief, is tantamount to printing money. When it sells, the procedure is reversed and money tends to drain out of the private economy. The securities traded are mainly Treasury issues of varying maturities.

Over the years, there has been far more buying than selling, and since the late 1960s, the money supply—cash plus most checking and savings deposits—has nearly quintupled. In the same interval, for perspective, the size of the economy, after adjusting for inflation, has risen by less than 70 percent.

This money-creating power clearly places the federal government under less pressure than other borrowers to balance the books. If there's a printing press in your basement that grinds out legal tender, why worry about trimming the household budget? The next dollar will be coming, whenever needed, from down below. One may reasonably wonder, in light of the federal money-making arrangement, why the government bothers to borrow at all and instead doesn't simply print money. The answer is that ruinous inflation, on the order of the German experience in the early 1920s, would surely ensue. However many problems it may cause, governmental borrowing doesn't bring with it the sort of inflationary pressures that simply printing money does. After all, the government can only borrow as much as lenders are willing to provide. Accordingly, the government will try to borrow as much as it possibly can, and only then will it resort to printing money.

Despite its ability to print money to pay its bills, the federal government faces an increasingly serious debt problem, one that may not seem as acute as that facing a consumer whose car is about to be repossessed or a company whose creditors are about to plunge it into bankruptcy, but deadly serious nonetheless. As its debt grows, the government must create money ever more rapidly. But as the money supply rises, prices will tend to rise as well. The reason is that as more and more dollars chase a relatively stable supply of goods and services, prices will be bid up by competing buyers. This is what takes place when money-supply growth persistently outstrips the rate at which business activity as a whole can grow. Money is easily produced, but goods and services require labor and material. The rate at which they can be furnished, in turn, depends on such imponderables as the size and skill of the labor force and the availability of resources. (Special factors can offset, at least for a while, the tendency of excessive monetary growth to generate inflation, as in the early 1980s, when slumping oil prices dampened the inclination of the general price level to increase in the wake of a sustained, sharp money-supply rise.)

The Federal Reserve, to be sure, can slow or even stop an expansion of the money supply. It can even reduce the money supply, for example, by selling large amounts of Treasury bills, a step that could serve to counteract inflation. But a reduction of the money supply could pose new problems, for the government soon could find itself unable to pay its debts—for instance, interest due on its various outstanding bonds, notes, and bills, to say nothing of refunding debt that has become due. The government, in the process, would find it difficult if not impossible to sell new issues of such securities. Among the many losers in such a scenario, in addition to the holders of Treasury securities, would be millions of individuals who depend on paychecks from the government, from military personnel to people on welfare to federal civilian employees in Washington and elsewhere. The government, in such circumstances, would largely cease to function.

In fact, between 1929 and 1933, when as much as 25 percent of the labor force was out of work, the money supply contracted by about one third and the Fed didn't grasp what was happening. The data were sketchy, and such institutions as the Federal Deposit Insurance Corporation (FDIC) hadn't yet been established. When banks failed, as thousands did, there was no governmental agency ready to resupply depositors' lost savings. With each new failure and subsequent loss of deposits, the money supply shriveled further, and further still as more and more people lost their jobs.[2]

Nowadays, of course, the monetary authorities at the Fed are keenly aware of each weekly wiggle of the money supply and continually track it in several forms, ranging from a rather narrowly defined version that includes mainly currency in circulation and checking-type accounts to a very broad version comprised as well of all sorts of savings deposits.

In light of the 1929–33 debacle, it's unthinkable that the policy-makers in Washington would again allow the money supply to shrink as it did then. But that's not really the question now. Because of the enormous rise in federal debt in recent decades, we now must wonder whether the Fed can safely slow the growth of the money supply to forestall inflation, consistent with the economy's capacity to expand over the long term. The potential for economic growth in the U.S. appears to be in the neighborhood of 3 or 4 percent annually —and not substantially higher, as some so-called supply-side economists assert. It follows logically that the money supply should also grow by 3 to 4 percent annually over the long term, but the huge pileup of government debt suggests that economic havoc would result if such a relatively slow rate of monetary expansion actually prevailed for very long. To pay its bills—including the costs of its huge entitlement programs —the government needs to expand the money supply at rates far greater than the economy's capacity to grow.

Occasionally, after several years of torrid increases in the money supply and some of the most severe inflation in our history, the Fed has attempted to slow monetary growth for protracted periods. For example, the rate of increase in the narrowly defined money supply, called M1, was progressively reduced between mid-1980 and mid-1982; from about 15 percent annually to a 1982 low of just under 3 percent, this adjustment brought the rate of gain safely within the economy's estimated ability to expand over the long term.

So far so good. But consider what else happened between 1980 and 1982. The economy underwent one of the severest slumps since the 1930s. For the first time in the postwar era, the unemployment rate moved into double digits as corporate profits plunged and failures soared. By mid-1982, with the money supply at last expanding at a rate deemed appropriate to the economy's growth potential, business activity seemed on the verge of collapse. The government was still paying its bills, but with the deepening slump and the consequent loss in tax revenues, the federal budget was toppling into a deficit that seemed ultimately to threaten federal solvency. Meanwhile, the debts of such nations as Mexico and Argentina became unmanageable as the recession in America deepened, constricting world trade. In order to service enormous debts incurred at banks in the U.S. and other industrialized countries, such less-developed nations depend heavily on funds earned through exporting various raw materials to the industrialized nations.

In the circumstances, the Fed had little choice. It did what had to be done and had not been done in the early 1930s. Starting in August 1982, monetary growth began to climb sharply. In June and July of that year, the M1 component of the money supply rose at annual rates of less than 3 percent. But in August, with the recession deepening, money-supply growth rose to more than 12 percent annually. Still larger gains followed. By October, the rate of increase topped 17 percent. And by November, not surprisingly, the recession finally began to abate. A vigorous business recovery followed. Unemployment subsided, profits climbed, and interest rates declined sharply, as usually happens in economic recoveries. Even inflation, which had abated as the recession deepened, remained relatively dormant, again a usual pattern as the economy moves up from a recessionary phase. In this regard, it's noteworthy that foreign purchases of U.S. government securities—in effect, foreign financing of the U.S. budget deficit—tended to raise the international value of the dollar, and this served to dampen inflation and hold down interest rates.

The Fed's action was a welcome change, even though in the longer run it must be viewed as little more than a holding action. Moreover, it was clear that the Fed's attempt to keep monetary growth in line with the economy's long-term potential to expand had failed. The federal deficit, moreover, remained awesome as the economy strengthened, diminishing only slightly as revenues picked up, for the Reagan administration had pushed through Congress a series of reductions in various tax rates, while permitting transfer payments and military expenses to grow. Federal spending continued to reach new highs, despite the much-publicized curtailment of such programs as the free school-lunch plan.

In 1985 alone, fifty-four new government-benefit programs were created, pushing the grand total to a record 1,013.

Insofar as the economy recovered from the 1981–82 slump, so-called supply-side economists, who urged the tax cuts on the theory that this would rekindle business activity, proved to be correct. But their additional forecast that the budget deficits would disappear as the country prospered was dead wrong. In a departure from the pattern prevailing in most earlier postwar upturns, the budgetary shortfall didn't come close to disappearing, for the deficit had grown so large before the recovery that even a vigorously rising economy proved insufficient to reduce it.

Since the late 1970s, the rise of federal debt has accelerated sharply—up 6 percent in 1979 and then ever more sharply until in 1982 the rate of increase reached a high of 19.4 percent. For a time in the earlier postwar years, as the economy expanded briskly, outstanding federal debt edged down in terms of the gross national product, the broadest gauge of overall business activity. But no more. At 27 percent of GNP as recently as 1981, the ratio has risen steadily—to 31 percent in 1982, 35 percent in 1983, nearly 37 percent in 1984.[3] The pattern seems to be continuing, so that by the end of the 1980s, several studies show, the debt level will approximate 50 percent of GNP. In 1985 alone, each taxpayer's share of the federal debt increased by $4,234, and each taxpayer's share of the interest due on this debt amounted to $2,175.

WHAT makes this accumulation of debt worrisome is the interest-payment burden that it places on the government and thus on individual American taxpayers. As recently as 1974, this burden came to less than $20 billion, or about $100 for each American. By the end of the 1970s, it was just over $40 billion. It reached $50.7 billion in 1980; $67.7 billion in 1981; $82.2 billion in 1982; $89.8 billion in 1983; and went above $100 billion in 1984. At that rate of gain, Uncle Sam's yearly interest burden would exceed $200 billion before the end of the decade, greater than the entire budget deficit only five years ago. A study by New York's Citicorp, which concludes that this interest-rate burden will "imperil economic stability," reckons that "by 2004 the [annual] deficit would top $1 trillion, the publicly held national debt would approach $12 trillion and the annual interest on that debt would be more than $1 trillion." A doomsday scenario.

These awesome numbers assume that the economy will grow year after year at an average annual rate of between 3 and 3.5 percent, approximately its long-term average. Even if the economy were to expand appreciably faster than that —even as rapidly as 5 percent each year—the budget would still be deep in red ink as late as 1996, according to Citicorp. But nothing remotely close to such a rate of growth over so long a period has ever happened in the U.S.

An analysis by Morgan Guaranty Trust Co. soon after President Reagan's reelection notes that "there is little conviction outside of [Reagan] administration circles that the U.S. can grow its way out of its budget problems." It argues—correctly, in my opinion—that the "administration's optimism" that the budget deficit can be significantly reduced by the end of the decade without major tax increases rests on unrealistic assumptions of economic growth over the next five years, averaging over 4 percent annually. The analysis correctly warns, as well, that federal borrowing to cover debt has reached dangerously high levels.

As recently as 1970–74, such borrowing amounted to about 15 percent of total U.S. savings, up from a yearly average of 5 percent in the preceding ten years. In 1975–79, this rate climbed above 25 percent, and in the first half of the 1980s, it averaged about 50 percent. Such a trend, the report concludes, underlies "the sense of concern about the deficit in financial markets." At the time, the economy had been expanding briskly for a full two years, in the wake of the severe 1981–82 recession, but only an increasing inflow of foreign funds kept the government's rising borrowing needs from causing severe financial strains. In 1984, for instance, 14 percent of federal borrowing was from lenders based abroad. That was up from a rate of 5 percent only two years earlier.

Meanwhile, the nonpartisan Congressional Budget Office (CBO) was warning that a huge budget deficit loomed for 1989—very probably exceeding $250 billion—even assuming a recession-free economy through the period and growth rates modestly higher than the long-term average of roughly 3 percent a year. The CBO projection also assumed that interest rates would remain flat or decline modestly through the period, hardly the expected pattern in such circumstances.

THE hard fact is that the government can cover its perennial deficits only in certain ways, all of which present difficulties.

First, through the Federal Reserve, it can print money to service its debt. But to do so willy-nilly would eventually cause ruinous inflation, destroying whatever value the dollar may retain, as money printing and inflation destroyed the German mark in the early 1920s. Second, the government can borrow even more heavily than it has been doing. But excessive borrowing tends to drive up interest rates in general, not simply on Treasury securities, and ultimately will stifle investments that foster economic growth. What's more, the more the government borrows, the more interest it eventually has to pay—an impossible situation. Third, the government can raise taxes and cut its own spending. But such actions, unless pursued with caution, will depress the economy, since each tends to restrict business activity. And fourth, the government can push through highly stimulative policies—typically, steep tax cuts and huge spending increases—to expand the economy so swiftly that the pace will generate sharply rising incomes and, in turn, sharply higher tax revenues. The problem is, however, that long before such sustained growth could be achieved, severe strains would surely develop to thwart healthy expansion; these would range from labor and material shortages to production bottlenecks to soaring interest rates.

Through a judicious combination of these strategies, it's perhaps possible that the deficit problem could be gradually corrected. But the Reagan administration, with its emphasis on the second and fourth alternatives, has succeeded only in increasing the deficit enormously. Reagan's successor will have to choose again, and the difficulties entailed in each alternative are unlikely to diminish in the interim.

Meanwhile, the nation sinks deeper and deeper into debt, and the collateral that supports the debt keeps eroding. Business activity rolls on, to be sure, but whatever gains occur increasingly rest on governmental stimulus and intervention to prevent proliferating financial trouble, and not on the sounder basis of accumulated savings, investments that foster future economic growth, and hard-earned productivity gains. Moreover, the message emanating from Washington is that no one can really get hurt in any of this, however shaky the loans may be, however misguided the investments are. And so the excesses continue to mount.

In essence, this expansion of federal debt, like the growth of individual and corporate debt, reflects again our tendency to live beyond our means and complements our diminishing propensity to save—a pervasive, disturbing pattern of extravagance. And there's yet another dimension to this pattern, one that receives less attention than borrowing or saving trends but that poses just as big a hazard for the economy as the 1990s approach.

THROUGH much of the generally prosperous period since World War II, while we have overborrowed and undersaved —so that for each American some $35,000 of debt is now outstanding—we've tended also to underinvest in the sort of facilities that serve in the long run to foster economic growth. In the long run, the economy's ability to expand depends on many variables, including the size and skill of the labor supply, the availability of materials, and the capacity and efficiency of plant and equipment. Throughout this century, as we've seen, America's annual economic growth has averaged about 3 percent. Of the factors that underlie this ability to expand over the long term, two—labor and materials—are relatively unaffected by undersaving and overborrowing. But production facilities have suffered mightily as a result of our extravagance.

The problem isn't so much underinvestment in general as underinvestment in facilities that provide not instant rewards, such as a new house, but longer-term benefits, such as a new factory. We have tended to overinvest in quick gratification. No other people in history have been as well housed as Americans. For all the well-founded concern about homeless individuals wandering the streets of New York, Los Angeles, and other large American cities, homeownership in America is unprecedented. In foreign eyes, it's awesome. While precise comparisons are unavailable, there's no question that the average American family's home is far larger, occupies more land, and is better built and equipped than comparable homes in any other major industrial country, even though, as we have seen, American goods generally are uncompetitive in world markets. An index measuring the size and quality of new homes in America, based on such considerations as square footage and amenities, was at a record high reading of 105 recently, up from 85 two decades ago and 95 in 1982.

This American lead in housing has been achieved, to a considerable extent, through governmental tax and spending measures that have channeled investment funds into real estate at the expense of new plant and equipment. As a percentage of gross national product, investment in new residential construction has ranged between 5 and 7 percent through much of the postwar period. That's sharply higher than comparable rates in the previous couple of decades, and it roughly matches the percentage of GNP recently invested in new plant and equipment; in the 1970s, for example, such outlays amounted to slightly over 6 percent of GNP. International data for the 1970s show that comparable plant-and-equipment investment rates were 12 percent in France and West Germany, 11 percent in Italy, 20 percent in Japan, and 8 percent in Britain. They further show that U.S. productivity growth in manufacturing, at 2.5 percent annually for the period, was also lowest among the six countries, lagging behind gains of 4.8 percent in France, 4.9 percent in both West Germany and Italy, 7.4 percent in Japan, and 2.9 percent in Britain.

Homeowners through the postwar era have been allowed to deduct mortgage interest and property taxes without paying taxes on the income they would in theory earn by "renting" their homes to themselves. Moreover, profits from the sale of owner-occupied homes have recently been free from all capital-gains taxes if the proceeds are rolled over into new homes within twenty-four months after the sale. In addition, $125,000 in capital gains has been exempted from taxation if the home seller is at least fifty-five years old and selling a primary residence. No other capital investment—however much it may ultimately serve to toughen the country's economic muscle—receives such kindly treatment. Notwithstanding, when the Congress began trying to "reform" the tax code in 1985, the various tax advantages for homeowners were largely untouched, while previously enacted incentives to invest in plant and equipment, such as the investment tax credit and liberalized depreciation rules, were eliminated or severely curbed.

Americans now are borrowing $120 to $140 billion a year to expand further the housing stock and construct office buildings (which are currently in oversupply, since investment in commercial real estate has long been a prime beneficiary of tax-sheltering legislation, recently corrected to a degree, that in some instances has allowed investors to deduct from their tax bills more than they actually have invested in particular projects). Meanwhile, the manufacturing industries on which we depend greatly to service our external debt are deteriorating.

HOUSING policy has also encouraged excessive indebtedness and overspending as more and more Americans have been putting their homes into hock, or into deeper hock as the case may be, in order to acquire countless other things, ranging from pleasure boats to vacation trips to Europe to country-club memberships. So long as home prices are rising, as they have through much of the postwar era, this use of home equity to finance the purchase of consumer goods and services has been a relatively painless way of increasing one's expenditures—in essence, consumption financed out of thin air rather than from hard work and saving.

Let's take a hypothetical case. In 1973, Mr. Jones buys a house for $50,000—twice his $25,000-a-year salary. He puts down $10,000 and obtains a twenty-five-year, 8 1/2 percent mortgage loan for the balance. The loan costs him about $325 a month—16 percent of his salary—but is tax deductible. In 1980, he sells the house for $100,000. Because he still owes some $35,000 on the mortgage, he nets $65,000, which a brokerage fee cuts to $59,000.

Then Mr. Jones buys a larger house for $150,000—three times his currently higher salary. Initially, he decides to put down $37,000, 25 percent of the price, and for the balance to take out a twenty-five-year, 14 percent loan costing about $1,300 monthly. Subtracting his down payment from his $59,000 sale proceeds, he would wind up with $21,500 in cash —what economists call realized home equity.

Mr. Jones could have added the $21,500 to the new down payment. But he asks himself whether the resulting reduction in his mortgage bill—some $250 a month—is worth giving up all the $21,500 to the bank. He decides that it isn't, particularly because mortgage payments are tax deductible. He compromises, using half that amount to trim his monthly payment to $1,175—28 percent of his salary, which he assumes will keep rising. He spends much of the rest of the money on a vacation in the south of France, fishing gear and golf equipment, and then invests what's left in rumba lessons and a trip to Disney World with the wife and kids.

In 1980, to take a year at random, there were some 4 million transactions of the sort involving the mythical Mr. Jones, and altogether they pumped some $20 billion into the spending stream. All the while, countless home-owning Americans moved deeper and deeper into debt. As for Mr. Jones, he has consumed abundantly, with his realized home equity, yet he has produced nothing and saved nothing, in sharp contrast with his counterpart, say, in Japan, who typically has put hard work and saving ahead of home buying and home hocking.[4]

In the inflation of the 1970s, housing prices on the average rose about 32 percent faster than the consumer price index. Over the postwar years, buyers of single-family houses have paid a total of $1.6 trillion for these homes, which in the early 1980s had a combined market value of about $2.6 trillion, or an unrealized capital gain of $1 trillion. Since 75 percent of all families own their own home, the rising real value of most housing in America through most of the postwar decades, according to Chase Econometrics, has "contributed greatly to the nation's general improvement in its standard of living."

Perhaps so. But there's also a large cost, for new spending means new debt, while savings—in this instance, the ultimate nest egg, one's home—have eroded in the process. Moreover, while debt has risen, funds that might have been invested in a more competitive economy have gone instead, to cite the case of Mr. Jones, for vacations in Provence. More distressing is that the coming generation of Americans won't be able to afford the standard of housing enjoyed by their parents, since their parents will have spent their inflated equity and left behind a mountain of debt. The pattern, it should be added, is apparent on the farm as well as in the home. To a considerable degree, excessive borrowing by farmers in recent years has reflected land speculation and the like rather than any effort to modernize facilities and reduce production costs. In the process, farms that might otherwise have remained within families, from one generation to the next, have instead landed on the auction block.

IN absolute terms, the standard of living in the U.S. is still the highest in the world. Economists have various ways of comparing living standards on a country-by-country basis. One is to compare gross national product on a per capita basis, adjusted for inflation. Another is to compare consumer expenditures, again on a per capita basis and again adjusted for inflation. Either way, the U.S. remains at the top, even though gains abroad have often been sharper. Data compiled by the Organization for Economic Cooperation and Development (OECD) show that Americans have 760 phones for every 1,000 citizens, while the comparable ratio in Britain is 524 per 1,000. Japan has 555 phones per 1,000; the Netherlands, 591; France, 600; West Germany, 599; Australia, 536; Italy, 426; Ireland, 253; Spain, 360; Greece, 355; Belgium, 430; and Canada, 654. Americans have 790 television sets per 1,000 population while, among other advanced nations, Sweden has 390 sets; Britain, 479; Switzerland, 378; France, 375; Italy, 243; and Japan, 556. The U.S. sports similar leads in automobiles, housing, and food consumption.

But in education, America is not ahead. Some 77 percent of Japan's fifteen-to-nineteen-year-old population is enrolled full-time in school or college, while the comparable U.S. rate is 72 percent. With only half the population of the U.S., Japan is producing about 50 percent more engineers each year. Studies show, moreover, that in twelve years of elementary and secondary education, the Japanese student actually receives four more years of schooling than his American counterpart, because of a more rigorous curriculum. There's good reason to argue that a Japanese high school diploma is the equivalent of an average American bachelor's degree.

LOOKING ahead, the President's Council of Economic Advisers has warned that there's a "great risk" that U.S. productivity growth "will continue to stagnate at low levels and that American workers will have to accept a lower growth rate in their standard of living than their foreign counterparts." The warning extends to American goods, which will increasingly "cease to be competitive on world markets." A yawning trade deficit suggests that this grim scenario is already unfolding.

At home, meanwhile, the Congressional Budget Office has estimated that it would cost some $53 billion per year nationwide for our highways, transit systems, sewer and water facilities, and airports to be made "adequate." A high percentage of the nation's bridges, for example, are in sore need of overhaul. In some cities, the rate is above 50 percent, with Buffalo, New York, at 59 percent and Rochester, New York, at 57 percent. In most instances, the bridges were found "to be either structurally deficient or functionally obsolete," according to a study by the Cleveland Federal Reserve Bank.

To appreciate the role of productivity here, let's take a worker in a factory turning out washing machines and let's suppose that he receives a 10 percent raise in his hourly pay. If his hourly production of washing machines also increases 10 percent, the employer's labor costs per washer produced remain unchanged and the employer feels under no pressure to raise his prices to protect his margin of profit. For many years after World War II, this is more or less what happened.

Pay increased year after year. But productivity—the hourly per-worker output of washers—increased approximately at the same rate as wages. In some years, the pay gains slightly exceeded the productivity advance, while in others productivity rose slightly faster than pay. In the end, year after year, per-unit labor costs remained about flat and one potential source of inflationary pressures remained dormant.

But since the late 1960s, pay increases have repeatedly exceeded productivity gains. In some recent years, U.S. workers have received 10 percent pay boosts while productivity has stayed flat, so that the per-unit expense of labor has risen 10 percent and producers have come under intense pressure to raise prices in order to offset climbing costs and protect profit margins. In the process, moreover, as prices have begun to climb, the value of pay increases has tended to be erased. And when that happens, living standards stay put or drop rather than increase, as would happen if pay were to rise faster than the general price level.

SYMPTOMS of the American tendency to underinvest in areas that will foster economic growth in the longer run are plentiful. In a recent five years, for example, U.S. steel producers replaced only 2 percent of their equipment annually, down from an already minuscule rate of 3 percent in the 1960s. At the start of 1984, only 35 percent of the nation's steel-making capacity used the relatively modern technique of continuous casting. The comparable rates were 87 percent in Japan and 75 percent in West Germany. Similar signs of factory obsolescence can be found in a broad array of U.S. industries.

A Conference Board study finds that the average age of capital equipment in the U.S., at about seven years, is roughly a year older than in Japan. And the gap is far greater for structures, such as factory space. The U.S. average of nearly fifteen years dwarfs the comparable Japanese average of some ten years. In 1978–83, according to the Conference Board, U.S. investment in capital projects in manufacturing industries rose at an average annual rate of 3.6 percent, compared with a 5.4 percent gain in Japan. U.S. investment in such other industries as public utilities, communications, and wholesale and retail trade also rose 3.6 percent annually in the period, far beneath the comparable 7.6 percent increase in Japan.

An ominous pattern, looking to the future, is the degree to which U.S. investment in research and development (R&D) has lagged behind. Civilian R&D spending in the U.S. has recently approximated only 1.8 percent of gross national product, according to OECD data. The comparable rates for Japan and West Germany are both about 2.5 percent. In the early 1960s, the U.S. rate about matched those of the other two countries. Other OECD data show, by no coincidence, that overall savings—at less than 3 percent—come to a far smaller fraction of national output in the U.S. than in Japan or West Germany. The Japanese savings rate is some six times the U.S. level, and the West German rate more than double.

IT'S no surprise that in recent expansion phases of the business cycle, inflationary pressures in the American economy, such as production bottlenecks and delivery problems, have begun to build at lower and lower levels of plant usage. In the early postwar years, such pressures rarely developed until U.S. factories, on the average, were operating at roughly 95 percent of full capacity. Lately, in contrast, these pressures have begun to surface when the plant-operating level has climbed to near 85 percent of capacity.[5] This is mainly a consequence of outmoded facilities, still theoretically counted as part of capacity, but pressed into actual use to meet rising demand as the economy keeps expanding.

To make matters worse, the U.S. spends far more than any other noncommunist nation on defense, expenditures which do little to improve living standards but contribute to inflationary pressures. Investing dollars, say, in bomb factories puts more money in the hands of thousands of workers who make the bombs but does nothing to increase the supply of goods and services available for consumption. It does nothing to provide more washing machines or refrigerators or other such items that bomb-production workers may wish to buy with money earned making bombs. This tends to fuel inflation, which ultimately tends to reduce living standards and render the country still less competitive in world markets. We could of course forgo such consumption for the sake of a strong defense by paying more in taxes to support our military obligation. But here, too, responsibility has given way to overindulgence.

The U.S. economy, moreover, is becoming increasingly service oriented. If America's steel plants are largely obsolete, it's often remarked, why worry? It's the service economy that counts, it's claimed; America has no rival in such service areas as health, finance, entertainment, and telecommunications, to name a few. This may be so, but in the longer term, if America is to maintain a position of economic and ultimately political leadership, it clearly cannot afford to lose its manufacturing base.

The way to avoid that isn't through a turn to protectionism, as happened in the depressed 1930s, but through a commitment by policy-makers to spur lagging investment in new production facilities. The problem with protectionism, of course, is that it ultimately tends to stifle international commerce in a world whose economies have grown increasingly close-knit. Import restrictions in one country, be it the U.S. or Outer Mongolia, eventually bring counterrestrictions elsewhere. The upshot is a general diminution of international trade and, in the end, a worldwide contraction of economic activity.

The swing to a service economy, it should also be noted, further inhibits productivity advances. People on the production line grow increasingly productive as their facilities are modernized and improved. But productivity in service-type jobs, as a rule, isn't so easily increased. How do you automate a haircut? The upshot is that service-type employment, which has soared in the postwar decades, is relatively impervious to the techniques of automation that can work so well, for example, on production lines. Not surprisingly, services also constitute the sector of the economy where inflation has proved most difficult to control over the years. Even so, in many service jobs, pay levels are far below levels in manufacturing—as any laid-off steel worker who winds up with a job at a fast-food restaurant can attest.

The extent of the services swing is such that service-type jobs now make up nearly three quarters of all jobs. For long-term perspective, it's worth recalling that in the 1920s, before the Great Depression took hold, roughly two thirds of all jobs were within the manufacturing sector.

An increasingly service-oriented economy is also marked by underinvestment, since the manufacturing sector is normally where such outlays are required. If the U.S. is an illustration, a service-run economy also encourages overborrowing, overspending, and undersaving. Indeed, the U.S. example suggests that a service economy is marked by overindulgence, which, as we will see, is ultimately self-limiting and cannot endure.

Chapter 3

The Gap Goes On

For years we have been outrageously overpaying ourselves, compared to what competing workers elsewhere earn for similar tasks. This disparity doesn't grab headlines in the way that, say, a huge federal-budget deficit can, partly because the precise pay gap is harder to quantify than statistics showing, for instance, the rate at which Americans save. Figures giving international comparisons of pay, fringe benefits, productivity, and other such matters are painstakingly constructed by an obscure unit within the Labor Department's Bureau of Labor Statistics, a section not given to conducting press conferences or issuing news releases every month. Yet few of the government's number mills turn out more important data.

What complicates these global pay comparisons is the degree to which the ever-shifting international value of the dollar affects the readings. Any serious effort to match, for instance, the hourly pay of a U.S. auto worker against that of his counterpart in Britain obviously requires that the respective earnings be expressed in either dollars or pounds. If the dollar is strong relative to the pound, this will tend to raise the U.S. worker's pay level compared to that of the British worker, and vice versa.

Despite the statistical difficulties, the data show that U.S. pay levels in most businesses have outstripped those elsewhere through much of the post-World War II era. Nor is it remarkable that the strength of the dollar in the wake of the 1981–82 recession served to widen the disparity. But it's striking to see that moderation of pay increases in the U.S. in recent years often hasn't matched pay restraint abroad, despite the well-publicized salary cuts and so-called give-backs in key U.S. industries ranging from autos to steel.

Headlines about give-backs and pay reduction in the U.S. in recent years have tended to obscure the fact that similar moves have occurred abroad. It would be comforting to report that the painful pay cuts that many U.S. workers have taken in recent years have trimmed or eliminated the broad gap that has long existed between U.S. and foreign pay levels, but that's not what has been happening; instead, the pay differential has widened.

The impression that American workers somehow came out of the 1981–82 slump in a leaner, more competitive position, relative to their foreign counterparts, unfortunately isn't true. Symptoms of America's hopelessly uncompetitive pay scales range from record-breaking U.S. trade deficits to continuing pressure on Congress and the White House to erect higher and higher barriers against goods and services supplied by foreigners.

The disparity between U.S. and foreign pay levels is sharpest in manufacturing, where the Labor Department has worked out precise industry-wide comparisons on a global basis. The data express hourly pay levels abroad as percentages of the U.S. average, including fringe benefits. All pay is calculated in U.S. dollars. The research shows that the hourly average comes to 75 percent of the U.S. rate in West Germany, 67 percent in the Netherlands, 56 percent in France, 58 percent in Italy, 46 percent in Britain, 50 percent in Japan, 9 percent in Brazil, 15 percent in Taiwan, 13 percent in Mexico, and 10 percent in South Korea. These disparities generally have been widening, though the dollar's decline on international currency markets after 1985 reversed the trend in some instances. As recently as 1981, Germany was at 97 percent of the comparable U.S. level, the Netherlands at 91 percent, France at 75 percent, Italy at 68 percent, Britain at

65 percent, Japan at 57 percent, Mexico at 34 percent, Brazil at 17 percent, and Taiwan at 14 percent. The Mexican peso was drastically devalued during the ensuing period.

In absolute terms, the hourly pay of U.S. production workers averaged $12.31 in 1984, a gain of 5.4 percent from a year earlier. If the dollar's appreciation isn't taken into account in the comparisons and the various pay increases are calculated simply in terms of each country's own currency, the 5.4 percent U.S. gain falls far short of the gains in such weak currency countries as Brazil (with a 119 percent hourly increase in the same twelve months) and Mexico (with a 56 percent gain). The hourly pay level in Brazil soared to 971.86 cruizeiros from 443.70, but in terms of the dollar, Brazil's hourly pay level plunged to $1.68 an hour from $2.47 a year earlier. Similarly, Mexico's hourly pay level rose to 224.93 pesos from 143.81, but in dollar terms it dropped to $1.45 from $1.97. But for all the talk of U.S. pay restraint, the U.S. rise of 5.4 percent outstrips the comparable gains in many areas, even when these increases are calculated in terms of particular currencies. It compares, for instance, with increases of 3.8 percent in the Netherlands, 4.3 percent in Japan, 4.7 percent in West Germany, and 5.2 percent in Taiwan.

Productivity advances tend to offset pay increases and thereby serve to hold down labor costs. But productivity has risen remarkably slowly in the U.S. through much of the postwar period. A Labor Department study of a dozen countries, mainly those noted above, finds that in a recent three years, productivity gains in the U.S. persistently lagged behind those for the twelve-nation group as a whole. By no coincidence, labor costs per unit of output have climbed relatively sharply in the U.S. In the early 1980s, the Labor Department analysis shows, U.S. labor costs rose some 12 percent faster than the average rise for the twelve countries. Even before taking the dollar's appreciation in those years into account, U.S. labor-cost increases exceeded those for such major competitors as Japan and West Germany.[1]

Lagging productivity gains would be less of a problem if the hourly output of U.S. workers were far higher than elsewhere in absolute terms, as was once the case but is no longer. A study of seven major countries finds that hourly output levels in West Germany, France, and Italy in the early 1980s were higher than in the U.S. and that levels in Japan and Canada were within less than one dollar of the U.S. figure. Only workers in Britain, at 61 percent of the U.S. level, produced far less per hour than their U.S. counterparts. In 1970, by contrast, the U.S. reading was appreciably higher than elsewhere.

In the U.S. airline industry, for example, average annual compensation in 1984 stood at about $43,000 per employee, some 8 percent higher than a year before, despite hefty pay cuts for employees of some airlines. Among the steepest was a wage reduction averaging $5,430 a year—part of a so-called wage-investment plan—taken by flight attendants at Eastern Air Lines. But even with that cut, to about $24,740 annually, the Eastern attendants remained on average nearly $6,000 above their British Airways counterparts, according to estimates by the London-based carrier, whose personnel took no pay cut.

A pattern of U.S. deterioration is evident even in industries where recent efforts to hold down pay have been extraordinary. U.S. auto workers submitted to multimillion-dollar pay reductions in the wake of the 1981–82 recession. As long after the recession as the summer of 1985, American Motors Corp. won a wage-cutting confrontation with six thousand workers at its two small-car producing plants in Wisconsin. After a month of bitter bargaining, the United Auto Workers union agreed to a broad package of wage reductions that AMC had been demanding as a condition for keeping its Kenosha and Milwaukee factories open. Among the union concessions were losses in seniority, overtime, and relief-time pay, as well as a wage cut of about 60 cents an hour from a $13.56 hourly base rate.

Notwithstanding such concessions, Labor Department data show that hourly pay of auto workers abroad, in terms of the comparable U.S. rate, remains relatively low–at 60 percent of the U.S. level in West Germany, 48 percent in Belgium, 41 percent in France and Japan, 39 percent in Italy, 31 percent in Britain, 19 percent in Brazil, and 9 percent in South Korea. Even so, the hourly pay of U.S. auto workers rose only 1.9 percent in 1983, to $19.02. That's less than half the comparable gain of 5.4 percent for U.S. manufacturing workers as a whole, but it still amounts to $6.71 an hour more than for U.S. production workers in general.

But that gap is relatively small. The U.S. auto-worker rate is $17.34 an hour more than that in South Korea. A South Korean auto worker would have to win an hourly pay increase of 21 percent to match, in dollar terms, the slim 1.9 percent gain—36 cents an hour—won in 1983 by U.S. auto workers. In fact, the South Korean pay level rose 5 percent, or 8 cents, in dollar terms and 11 percent in terms of the won, the South Korean currency unit.

As recently as 1981, the U.S. rate was somewhat less out of line with levels elsewhere. The hourly rate was 77 percent of the U.S. level for auto workers in West Germany, 76 percent in Belgium, 52 percent in France, 45 percent in Britain, 44 percent in Japan and Italy, and 18 percent in Brazil. Thus, the pay disparity widened everywhere, even though the U.S. auto industry endured a severe slump and massive layoffs.

Using similarly constructed pay data, the Labor Department finds that hourly steelworker pay comes to 59 percent of the U.S. rate in Belgium, 55 percent in the Netherlands and Japan, 51 percent in West Germany, 44 percent in France and Italy, 37 percent in Britain, 11 percent in South Korea, and only 8 percent in Brazil. As in the auto industry, the disparity has widened. In 1981, the readings were 80 percent in Belgium, 66 percent in the Netherlands, 61 percent in West Germany, 57 percent in Japan, 51 percent in France, 46 percent in Italy, 45 percent in Britain, and 14 percent in Brazil. The pattern persisted even though American steel, like the U.S. auto industry, underwent a severe recession.

Studies of other occupations show a similar pattern. The annual after-tax pay of a New York grade-school teacher with ten years of experience averages $20,100, according to one survey, while the comparable pay is $8,600 in Amsterdam, $1,000 in Cairo, $7,900 in London, $2,500 in Mexico City, $8,000 in Stockholm, $3,900 in Tel Aviv, and $15,300 in Tokyo. The take-home pay of an electrical engineer with five years' experience in Houston averages $26,600, compared with $13,600 in Düsseldorf, $3,100 in Manila, $10,900 in Milan, $10,300 in Rio de Janeiro, and $21,600 in Zürich. And so it goes, in occupation after occupation.[2]

THE disparity in pay is even more pronounced at the managerial level. Upper-echelon managers in the U.S. receive far more, on the average, than such managers elsewhere. In the auto industry, for example, the pay a top executive gets is thirty-six times the pay of his blue-collar counterpart, one study shows, while the Japanese auto executive gets about seven times the pay of his blue-collar counterpart.

In 1984, a year when U.S. wages rose relatively modestly and some production workers actually took pay cuts, top executives in banking—a business marked by the highest failure rate since the Great Depression—showed gains in total compensation, salary plus bonus, of 14 percent. Increases for top executives averaged 11 percent in manufacturing, another troubled sector that increasingly has turned to Washington for help of various sorts. For chief executive officers in manufacturing, bonuses averaged 56 percent of their salary in 1984, up from 50 percent the year before.

Among top executives at the nation's 337 largest companies, 48 earned at least $1 million yearly, and another 110 netted from $700,000 to $1 million. Only one of the 986 executives earned less than $100,000 a year, and only 76 earned under $200,000. For the group as a whole, pay rose about 15 percent, dwarfing the comparable pay gain for U.S. workers generally.

While the chieftains of U.S. corporations typically belong to a dozen or so country clubs, have several homes and company jets, helicopters and stretched limousines at their disposal, their counterparts in such places as Japan live far more simply. The home near Tokyo of one Japanese chief executive recently profiled in a U.S. magazine resembled the sort of house that might belong to a middle manager of a U.S. company. It was planted on about a half acre of land, had only three bedrooms, and was surrounded by a wire-mesh fence of the sort often seen in blue-collar neighborhoods on the outskirts of industrial cities in America.

A 1985 survey of remuneration in most major countries found that on the average, the annual pay of American executives was at least twice that of their counterparts abroad. The British executive's average pay was only 38 percent of the average U.S. executive. The comparable reading for French executives was 46 percent and for West German executives 54 percent.[3]

Both Owen Bieber, president of the United Auto Workers, and Secretary of Labor William Brock have called the pay grab of U.S. executives obscene and warned that in the longer run it can only lead to stiffer pay demands by rank-and-file workers in a wide range of industries.

A 1984 report in *The New York Times* lists as many as forty-six high-level executives, many of them a notch or two below the top, whose yearly compensation was above $1 million. Four of these were employed at automobile companies —two at General Motors and two at Ford—whose U.S. operations were still recovering from the 1981–82 recession and whose U.S. sales were being protected by a so-called voluntary quota system designed to keep out Japanese autos. The chief executive of General Motors alone received nearly $1.5 million, and right behind him was Ford's top man, with about $1.4 million—outrageous compensation in global terms.

An editorial-page article in *The Wall Street Journal,* appearing at about the same time, remarked that "the expansion and sweetening of bonus plans, and the distribution of virtually every penny permitted under current bonus formulas, are peculiar strategies for companies seeking wage restraint from workers; in Detroit, it is a refreshingly logical fact of life that big bonuses lead to big wage demands," and adds that a top Ford official, defending his own million-dollar-plus bonus, maintains that all the Ford officers' bonuses and salaries for 1983 added only some $4 to the cost of each car and truck produced during the year by the company. "There was a time in Ford's accounting labs," the editorial adds, "when a cost of a few dollars a car was a big deal. Remember the $6.65 a car that reputedly could have built a safer fuel system in the Ford Pinto?"

How, in light of their own bosses' pay, can American workers be expected to make the sort of sacrifices necessary to become globally competitive? Their bosses are greedily lining their pockets, yet pay cuts and give-backs are urged of them as part of a national effort to pare the huge U.S. trade deficit and strengthen Uncle Sam's stance in world markets. Since 1975, the average pay of chief executive officers of American companies has risen more than 160 percent, compared to increases of 110 percent for U.S. middle managers and less than 90 percent for lower-echelon personnel.

Relatively high pay levels in major U.S. manufacturing industries are often linked to the fact that unions tend to be relatively strong in such industries in the U.S., but unions tend to be even stronger abroad. The portion of the British work force belonging to unions stands at about 47 percent, more than twice the U.S. rate of nearly 20 percent. In Japan, 30 percent of the work force is unionized. In West Germany and the Netherlands, the rates exceed 40 percent, and in

Sweden, 90 percent. Clearly, a lot more than simply union-ism underlies our excessive pay rates.[4]

It is a practice particularly among American unions to keep older workers and lay off younger ones when business is slow, so there is little reason for union officials to worry about layoffs that might result from excessive pay demands. Steel workers, for instance, retain their voting rights for only two years after being furloughed. As a result, hundreds of thousands of out-of-work steel workers no longer have a voice in deciding whether or not any new pay demand should be pursued to a point of risking more jobs. Similarly, auto workers who have been let go retain their union voting rights for only six months after their jobless benefits have run out. After that, their voting rights must be renewed on a monthly basis, through time-consuming administrative procedures that discourage many members from remaining eligible to vote.

FOR years after World War II, the U.S. managed to sell more goods and services abroad than it imported, evidence of our ability to compete against all comers. But eventually these surpluses dwindled, until in 1972, for the first time in the postwar era, the U.S. ran a trade deficit, amounting to slightly less than $8 billion. But this deficit marked a disturbing change from the early postwar years, when the nation's balance of trade was in surplus, often by yearly amounts exceeding $25 billion and once, in 1947, by more than $45 billion.

The trade balance returned to a surplus position in 1973 and remained there until 1977, when the second of the postwar deficits developed. This time the shortfall was large, approximating $40 billion, and another, still larger, deficit occurred in 1978. The balance returned to surplus in 1979–81, but then the situation deteriorated drastically. By late 1984, the shortfall in trade was running at record annual rates exceeding $100 billion.

The response to this deterioration as it progressed in the early 1980s wasn't the logical one—to slash costs and spur productivity with an eye to providing world markets with cheaper, higher-quality goods and services. Instead, industries from textiles to motorcycles to steel lobbied, with considerable success, to exclude from the American marketplace cheaper, higher-quality products made abroad. The country that had championed freedom of international trade through much of the postwar era—when, conveniently, its own trade balance was in healthy surplus—was turning increasingly protectionist.

President Reagan was responsible during his first term for a variety of protectionist measures that limited foreign access to U.S. markets in such key industries as automobiles, steel, and textiles. But that by 1984 Reagan should emerge as the more free trade-minded of the two presidential candidates is striking evidence of how protectionist-minded the country had grown by mid-decade. Walter Mondale, the Democratic candidate, was still more sympathetic than Reagan to protectionism, endorsing for example a proposal mandating that all automobiles sold in the U.S. be made largely of U.S.-produced parts, the so-called domestic-content proposal.

Protectionism, in essence, represents still another attempt to live beyond our means, by barring foreign competition rather than undertaking the belt-tightening and hard work necessary for beleaguered U.S. industries to become competitive. Protectionist measures would doubtless be still more widespread were it not for the fact that protectionism is so clearly inflationary. The Reagan administration's effort to beat down the dollar's international value, launched in 1985 with the help of four other industrial nations, represents a relatively subtle form of protectionism, for as the dollar cheapens in foreign-exchange markets around the world, foreign goods and services grow costlier for Americans, just as if we had imposed a system of import tariffs and quotas. An incidental result of protectionism, whatever form it takes, is of course inflation, as imported goods on which we increasingly depend become relatively more costly.

Unlike the automobile, steel, or textile industries, the machine-tool business in the early 1980s was still largely unprotected by quotas, import duties, or other such measures. Perennially, since American toolmakers sold far more abroad than foreign tool producers sold here, U.S. firms were unprotected by import restraints. But by the late 1970s, more and more U.S. companies were finding that they could buy cheaper, better machine tools abroad, especially in Japan. Unrestricted by protectionism, U.S. imports of machine tools rose from $401 million in 1977 to $1.3 billion in 1982, or about one third of the U.S. market. As the percentage kept rising, protectionist sentiment increased apace in this once competitive industry.

In 1976, the average hourly output of Japanese machine-tool workers was some 20 percent lower than that of their U.S. counterparts, and the Japanese clung to a relatively harmless 3 percent of the total U.S. market. By 1982, however, Japan's productivity had risen to twice that for the U.S., and its share of the American market had quadrupled, to 12 percent. Moreover, labor rates for the Japanese machine-tool workers were 40 percent lower than American rates.

The National Machine Tool Builders' Association has repeatedly petitioned the government for relief from imports, citing Section 232 of the Trade Act of 1962, the national security clause, but the industry's small size in relation to tool-consuming industries, particularly automotive companies, makes action unlikely. These relative giants would be hurt if such legislation resulted in higher prices, slower delivery times, or a generally less competitive, less innovative marketplace for machine tools. U.S. machine-tool makers will probably never receive the full degree of protection that they want. But some assistance seems likely, on the ground that national defense is involved. Senator Robert Dole of Kansas, the former majority leader, has said that "nothing in our defense establishment can be built without machine tools," adding that "they are obviously essential to our national defense. How can we tolerate a situation where we must depend on foreign suppliers for such critical items? To do so would obviously weaken our defense capabilities." In late May 1986, Reagan finally directed his trade negotiators to begin talks with Japan and several other countries to seek "voluntary" restraint agreements on various machine tools, with the warning that curbs would be the alternative.

IN 1962, imported cars accounted for 4.9 percent of new-auto sales in the U.S. The comparable rate in the early 1980s was in the neighborhood of 30 percent. The rise of imports over the postwar years would have been far steeper had the Japanese auto makers not been forced to limit their sales by U.S. threats of an outright ban of car imports. The restraint program, though labeled voluntary, was anything but, and its demise in early 1985 represented a rare—and short-lived— step away from protectionism. The restraints were reinstituted in 1986, as the Japanese became increasingly fearful of outright U.S. protectionism.

In 1980, the U.S. car industry appealed for "temporary protection" from Japanese imports, and in 1981, President Reagan announced that an agreement had been reached with Japan on "voluntary export restraint" that would limit Japanese automobile exports to the U.S. to about 1.7 million cars per year, a decision that aroused little opposition since it followed a year in which U.S. automobile makers lost about $4 billion and employment in the industry had fallen by more than 20 percent, due partly to a sharp rise in demand for imports. Moreover, Chrysler had recently been rescued from bankruptcy by federally backed loans. Thereafter, these "voluntary" quotas were tightened. As a result, the price of imported Japanese cars then began to climb, by an average of $920 to $960 per car in 1981–82 alone.

The average price of a new car between the introduction of the quota arrangement and mid-1984 rose nearly $2,000, benefiting Japanese producers and their dealers by at least $2 billion per year. As for American consumers, the average per-car sales price was some $800 higher than if the restraint program had not been launched. The cost to American consumers works out to about $160,000 annually per auto-worker job saved. "Employment creation at this cost is surely not worth the candle," concludes one study, questioning a program that "turns on whether Americans wish to pay large premiums on their cars in order to increase the employment of auto workers at wages far above the manufacturing average." It finds no evidence that the quota arrangement advanced the competitiveness of the U.S. auto industry.[5]

A footnote: While hourly employment costs in the U.S. auto industry are some 60 percent higher than the average for all U.S. manufacturing concerns, such costs in Japan's auto industry are only 25 percent higher than Japan's all-manufacturing average. It would be comforting to believe that through belt-tightening and brisker productivity gains, the U.S. auto industry may once again become competitive. But this hardly seems in prospect. Auto-industry productivity in Japan is about two and a half times greater than in the U.S., even though the auto workers there, as we have seen, earn far less.

Again, self-indulgence of this sort is self-limiting. American automobile makers may not sanction protection for American machine-tool producers, but the American public also won't continue to sanction the degree of protection—and the higher prices—in the car industry that Detroit would like to see.

THE American steel industry provides a particularly sorry illustration of how protectionism fails in the longer run to salvage businesses unwilling to regain their competitive position through fundamental reform. Though steel receives considerable protection against competition from abroad and was once the backbone of industrial America, the steel business has been in serious difficulty with import competition for even longer than autos. Not only have imports eroded demand for steel made in the U.S., but the importance of steel, unlike autos, is in a long-term decline. Since the mid-1950s, the consumption of steel-mill products has dwindled in terms of overall economic activity. At that time, about 125 tons of steel were consumed in the country for every $1 million of gross national product. Now, with plastics and other lighter, more flexible substitute materials, only about fifty tons of steel are used per $1 million of GNP.

Despite all their problems, however, America's steel producers have done relatively little to pare their costs and make their industry more competitive. American steel workers are far more highly paid than steel workers elsewhere, and the disparity has been widening. According to the Chicago Federal Reserve Bank, "Repeatedly, the industry has sought solutions to its problems through protection against foreign competition and the government has obliged." In the short run, governmental measures to limit or stop sales of foreign-made steel in the U.S. may tend to benefit the U.S. steel industry—for example, by enabling the industry to raise prices and increase production, employment, and profits. But the Chicago Federal Reserve Bank warns that "the cost of these benefits will be borne by U.S. consumers and by workers and producers in other industrial sectors of the U.S. economy." Other indirect costs will ultimately fall on such developing nations as Brazil, Mexico, and South Korea. A reduction in their ability to export will impede their capacity to import U.S. products and to service their debt to U.S. banks.

Protectionism will eventually hurt a wide range of U.S. exports as well as an already troubled U.S. banking system, which holds much of the debt of such countries as Brazil and

Mexico. Data compiled by the Congressional Budget Office place the cost of steel protection to U.S. consumers at about $180,000 per job saved, hardly a sensible arrangement.

Meanwhile, the Trade Policy Center, a research group based in London, has put the expense to American consumers of tariffs designed to protect U.S. manufacturers of textiles and apparel at some $12 billion yearly. Similarly, federal statisticians estimate that U.S. consumers paid at least an extra $700 million annually during a recent five-year period because of protectionism in the footwear business.

Studies of the Great Depression leave little doubt that the 1930s slump was deepened and prolonged by protectionist moves to limit the flow of foreign-made merchandise into the U.S. The so-called Smoot-Hawley Tariff Act, passed in 1930, turned a severe recession into something far worse. Smoot-Hawley increased import duties in most major industries, particularly in minerals, chemicals, dyestuffs, and textiles. It was passed over the strenuous objections of the American Bankers Association and a group of 1,028 leading economists, whose warnings were soon proved correct. Within two years of the signing, twenty-five other countries had established retaliatory tariffs. International trade shriveled, and the world slump kept deepening.

A sharp swing by the U.S. to protectionism now would surely trigger painful countermeasures abroad. In the European Common Market, where fully half of all economic activity relates to foreign trade, the likely retaliation would be against the already beleaguered American farmers, who have recently been shipping about $3 billion yearly of fats, oils, and animal feed to the Common Market area.

An editorial in *The Washington Post* appearing in late 1984, when the U.S. trade deficit first moved appreciably above $100 billion a year, said: "Of all the symptoms of rising instability in the American economy, none is less noticed . . . than the deficit in foreign transactions [and] none is more dangerous. . . . Most of the people who matter in American politics and business learned their economics at a time when the rest of the world hardly mattered to this country's prosperity."

The main pressure for still more protectionism emanates from the country's leadership ranks. A survey in 1985 of 295 major corporations, most of them in manufacturing, found that nearly two thirds advocate still more protectionist measures by the government. Three quarters of the companies reported that they have lobbied hard for such help.

As a percentage of gross national product, imports have risen from about 5 percent in 1975 to more than 10 percent in recent years, while foreign trade as a whole has risen from 6.7 percent of GNP in 1960–65 to 15.9 percent in 1978–84. Unquestionably, the rest of the world matters very much nowadays in this country's prosperity. The sagging trade balance and demands for still greater protectionism are yet another sign of America's tendency to live beyond its means.

Chapter 4

Nothing Works

There is, unfortunately, no economic prescription to deal in an orderly fashion with the trouble that is emerging from our ingrained tendencies—our determination—to borrow too heavily, to insist on too much pay for too little work and, whenever things don't turn out, to look to Washington for instant relief. The situation evolving now goes beyond the help that any economic theory, or set of theories, can give. Just as meteorological theories are of no help once a hurricane is bearing down on your home, no economic theory can help once the underlying economic environment has become as troubled as it now is.

A common supposition is that Thomas Carlyle called economics the dismal science because it appears, at least to some observers, such an indistinct, uninteresting business, full of ifs and maybes. But that's not the meaning that the Scot intended. Rather, he regarded economics in the other sense of dismal: showing or causing gloom or depression. Economics, to Carlyle, was a science whose study led to the conclusion that prosperity inevitably would diminish, while financial misery just as surely would spread.

But since World War II, economic policy has mainly reflected a series of highly optimistic theories, none suggesting in the least that prosperity must diminish, and in fact in much of the world prosperity has grown remarkably since the war. But the optimism is shallow, for none of the various economic theories that seek to account for prosperity since the war really holds up. So long as we were able to live beyond our means with impunity, this didn't much matter. But now it begins to matter very much. Unfortunately, none of the economic ideas that have dominated the postwar decades appears to hold an answer.

Chronologically, the first and probably the most important of these economic theories is the fiscalist concept, inspired by the writings of John Maynard Keynes, which stresses the importance of taxes and governmental spending and argues that governments have the power to stimulate or suppress economic activity, as the need arises. Specifically, Keynesian theory urges that government spending be stepped up during recessions, even if an appreciable budget deficit happens to be among the consequences of such stimulative measures. A corollary to this notion is the danger of a so-called liquidity trap, which may develop when money is pumped into public hands but is saved and not spent. As savings pile up, the economy noses down on account of lackluster spending.

The Keynesian solution, as it has often been applied by policy-makers in postwar American recessions, is for Uncle Sam to spend until business recovers. According to this theory, tax reduction tends to stimulate the economy, by leaving more money in the hands of consumers, while tax increases work the opposite way.

In this so-called fiscalist view, therefore, federal budgets needn't always be near a balanced position. Deficits, achieved through higher federal spending and tax reductions, are seen as highly beneficial in times—usually during recessions or the early stages of business recoveries—when the economy is operating substantially below its potential level.

Conversely, budget surpluses, according to fiscalists, are appropriate when the economy is running close to flat out. Ideally, the surpluses will materialize as tax revenues climb along with incomes, while governmental outlays for unemployment compensation and welfare diminish amid increasing prosperity. If such natural tendencies prove insufficient

to temper the economy's rise and prevent inflationary pressures, the fiscalist prescription calls for such active measures
as tax increases and federal spending cuts.

The intended result of such a policy is an economy that
expands steadily, avoiding both recessions and inflation. But
this is far from what has actually happened. Recessions, some
of them severe indeed, have repeatedly marked the postwar
record, along with surges of inflation.

In practice, the fiscalist idea of how the economy ought to
work has failed, perhaps, as its proponents have argued, because policy-makers in Washington haven't followed the
theory closely enough. According to the fiscalists, the outstanding failure was President Johnson's effort to pay for the
war in Vietnam by grinding out money through the Federal
Reserve, rather than raise taxes. Had the economy been in
a recession at the time, this guns-plus-butter approach would
no doubt have been less deleterious. But by 1965, when the
decision was taken, the economy had been expanding for
nearly half a decade and Johnson's costly Great Society
spending programs were already under way. As a result, the
additional monetary stimulation, without a tax boost, accelerated inflation, brought the highest interest rates since
the war, and created a variety of new economic dislocations,
ranging from labor shortages to production bottlenecks.

The Johnson administration was guilty of extreme economic mismanagement. But even if it weren't, there's little
evidence that fiscalism ever really worked as planned. As
Arthur Burns told me years ago, when he was chairman of
the Federal Reserve Board, fiscalist ideas of economic management simply aren't "viable policy for our country." Burns
added that "confidence in Keynesian ideas began collapsing
in the 1970s."

The record bears Burns out. Fiscalist theory has always
held, for instance, that high interest rates preclude brisk
economic growth, but the strong business upturn that began
in late 1982 occurred despite exceedingly high interest rates.

As the 1981–82 recession was ending, fiscalist economists predicted that the upswing would be feeble and brief, but it proved to be vigorous and sustained.

The large budget deficits, which reflect high levels of federal spending in proportion to what the government collects in taxes, should reduce unemployment, according to fiscalist theory. Yet the jobless rate has generally been higher as the postwar deficit has grown than when the budget was more nearly in balance. Also according to the theory, federal spending, which has grown far more rapidly in recent decades, should have brought more growth and minimal joblessness, but this has not happened.

There's no simple explanation of why fiscalist theory hasn't worked. According to the theory, the federal budget should swing into healthy surplus, for example, once recessions end and the economy and, most importantly, federal revenues are again on the increase. But in recent decades, the budget has remained deeply in deficit long after recessions have ended. The essential difficulty is that today's economy has become so severely out of kilter that neither the fiscalist prescription nor any other can readily set things right. When federal borrowing, for instance, is already so great that it repeatedly threatens to swamp the nation's credit markets and when interest payments on the federal debt become a major, ever-mounting item of expense in the federal budget, any plan for a sharp rise in federal spending to spur economic growth may deter rather than encourage business activity. If the fiscalist notion really worked, the economy by all rights should have been rising briskly through much of the past quarter century, with the budget in overall balance. Instead, there have been repeated recessions and the budget has been awash in red ink.

BUT no other theory of economic management has proved any better than fiscalism, though proponents of other strategies may claim otherwise. For instance, industrial policy was much in the news in the early stages of the Reagan-Mondale 1984 presidential election campaign. A Mondale adviser, Professor Robert Reich of Harvard, urged the adoption of industrial policy to avert economic trouble. The basis of industrial policy is that central planning by the federal government can lead to a stronger economy, that Washington's bureaucrats are best able to manage the economy, notwithstanding its awesome diversity. In the late 1970s, Senator Hubert Humphrey argued that too much economic planning "is done by private corporations" and that "there is little coordination among the many independent private planning efforts." He contended that federally managed economic planning was the best route toward the "nation's goals" of price stability and full employment.

At around the same time, Robert Heilbroner of New York's New School for Social Research felt that the planning process should resemble the legislative process. It was inefficient, he felt, that the flow of goods from factory to factory or from factory to customer, the entrance of labor and capital into particular businesses or their exit, should be "largely entrusted to profit-seeking, competitive ways of the accustomed market mechanism." Central planning in such circumstances may not be a panacea, he conceded, but all things considered, "in the end . . . planning offers hope" for the economy that cannot be found elsewhere. Ray Marshall, President Carter's secretary of labor, went further, claiming that the twin problems of inflation and joblessness plaguing the economy during much of the 1970s seemed sure to worsen without more federal planning. "One of the basic problems we have," he warned, "is unregulated and unplanned market forces." But the sharpest drop in inflation in recent decades came not during Secretary Marshall's term but under the Reagan team, with its well-publicized disdain for industrial policy.

The drop followed a severe recession, in 1981–82, and a

prolonged period of monetary restraint by the Federal Reserve, and not the implementation of any industrial policy.

To understand the fallacy of industrial policy, a good place to start is with the Austrian economist and Nobel laureate Friedrich Hayek, who has long objected to the idea of central planning precisely because America's economy is so vast and diverse. "We hope by central direction," he observes, "to achieve . . . efficiency in the use of resources which the market makes possible," but this is "clearly impossible—simply because [of] the very complexity of the . . . modern economic system." It's not possible, in his view, that "any one mind or planning authority could possibly survey the millions of connections between the ever more numerous interlocking separate activities which have become indispensable for the efficient use of modern technology." So far, he seems to be right.

Harvard's Reich contends that "America [has] lacked any mechanism to accelerate economic change." But the mechanism that Mr. Reich suggests—government guidance of market forces—seems a dubious remedy. Today's sad reality, as noted in a Heritage Foundation study, is that "the ability to understand the intricacies of government actions and rules can do more to enhance a firm's profitability than most farsighted research programs; the political influence to obtain subsidies or protection can be much more important than meeting foreign competition." In other words, industrial policy is already in place, to a degree, and it clearly isn't working.

MONETARISM is the other dominant economic theory to emerge since the Second World War, and it argues that sustained economic growth depends largely on how the Federal Reserve handles monetary policy, that the Fed control the money supply so that it grows at a steady rate, consistent with the economy's own capacity to expand from year to year, which studies place in the neighborhood of 3 to 4 percent annually over the long term.

Monetarist economists blame much of the economy's troubles—the frequent recessions and surges of inflation—on inconsistent Fed policy, just as the fiscalists blame the failure of their theory on poor political decisions. The leading monetarist is Milton Friedman, the Nobel laureate from the University of Chicago. A harsh critic of the Fed's management of monetary growth through much of the postwar period, Friedman believes that money matters most and assigns a relatively minor role to federal spending and tax policy.

But monetarism is as simplistic as fiscalism. As the fiscalist Walter Heller has put it, "Milton Friedman's ideas are wonderful, but unfortunately they work only in heaven," to which one might reply that Heller's ideas won't work even in heaven. How can the Federal Reserve maintain a steady growth of the money supply at 3 to 4 percent, year in and year out, no matter what Congress chooses to spend and no matter what tax policy the White House pursues? Moreover, exactly how should the money supply be measured? Can the Fed really regulate monetary growth so finely? Most importantly, is the relationship between monetary growth and the expansion of overall business activity really so closely linked?

Money supply isn't easily defined. It comes in various shapes and sizes. First, there's M1, consisting mainly of checking-account deposits and currency in circulation. Then there's M2, which embraces all of M1 plus various savings-account deposits. And finally there's M3, which comprises both the narrower Ms plus certain large savings deposits and institutional money-market accounts. There's also a so-called monetary base, which is narrower than any of the Ms and consists of bank reserves plus currency. Most monetarists maintain that M1 is the monetary measure that the Fed should keep its eye on, that M1 money is "transactional" in that it's the sort that most likely changes hands when business is conducted. But not all monetarists agree that M1 is the gauge that should be regulated. Some monetarists opt for M2 or even M3, because they are broader than M1. And some monetarists maintain that the monetary base is paramount because it's comprised of bank reserves, the "raw material" from which transactional money derives and multiplies under the country's system of banking.

A further complication is that the definitions of the various money supplies keep changing. In the early postwar period, money-market mutual funds didn't exist and therefore weren't a part of any M. Now they constitute a huge chunk of M2. Yet many monetarists believe that they rightly belong in M1 because holders often use such accounts—which increasingly offer check-writing privileges—to pay daily bills, small ones as well as large.

But even if it were pristinely clear which money measure should be regulated by the Fed, it's exceedingly unclear that the Fed is up to such a task. The record shows that none of the Ms has expanded consistently at rates remotely close to the economy's estimated long-run potential of 3 to 4 percent. Since President Johnson's fiscal mismanagement of the mid-1960s, monetary growth has tended to exceed the economy's long-run potential by a wide margin, and efforts to bring the various monetary growth rates into closer line with economic reality have usually ended in recessions, as happened in mid-1982, when the Fed slowed the rapid growth in M1 to an annual rate of less than 3 percent. As the resulting slump deepened and the Mexican debt crisis threatened some of the largest U.S. banks, the Fed quickly reversed field. By late that year, M1 was soaring at double-digit rates. In the fall of 1982, near the start of the economic recovery, M1 rose as much as 14 percent annually, a rate of gain rarely reached in the postwar era.

Further complicating the Fed's task is the matter of velocity. There's no question that the money supply—whichever version one chooses—is an important factor in the economy's behavior. But the rate at which the money supply turns over or, to put it more simply, changes hands—what economists call monetary velocity—can have an equally important influence. A 1 percent rise in the turnover of money has the same stimulative effect on the overall economy as a 1 percent increase in the money supply. Monetary velocity can be precisely calculated by dividing the gross national product by the money supply. The sum of money-supply expansion and velocity growth adds up to the rate of growth in the gross national product. Thus, a 1 percent rise in velocity plus a 3 percent rise in money-supply growth will combine to produce a 4 percent rise in GNP.

The problem is that a number of factors, quite apart from the money supply, can affect velocity, which tends to grow more rapidly when the economy is in an expansion phase and more slowly, or actually fall, in recessions. This is because during up phases of the cycle, consumers generally feel more carefree and, accordingly, attempt to get along with smaller balances of money in the bank per dollar of spending. The upshot is that money changes hands more quickly.

Financial innovation can also influence velocity. The introduction of such items as credit cards and overdraft facilities at thrift institutions induces people to finance more of their outlays using smaller bank-deposit balances. The tendency, again, is to increase monetary velocity. All in all, velocity is a gossamer concept, difficult for Washington's policy-makers to pinpoint, follow, or allow for in their deliberations over how the money supply should be managed.

The propensity of Washington to spend more than is collected in taxes also hampers the Fed's pursuit of a workable monetary policy. Consider the difficulty posed by perennial federal-budget deficits. When a deficit occurs, the Treasury Department is normally compelled to borrow funds in order to make up the government's financial shortfall. The Treasury can compete for money in the so-called open market, seeking to divert investors' funds that might otherwise be loaned, say, to a private corporation also in need of funds.

Such competition obviously tends to drive up interest rates and, ultimately, slows economic activity. Under law, the Federal Reserve may also purchase or sell government securities, which is the main way in which the Fed tries to control the money supply. When the Fed buys, it pumps funds into the economy, since it pays for its purchases with what amounts to newly created money; when the Fed sells Treasury issues, this tends to drain money out of the economy, as the various buyers pay the Fed.

In practice, when the Fed fears that the Treasury's borrowing needs are likely to force interest rates too high in the open market, it may decide to purchase some or all of the securities that the Treasury is trying to sell to cover the budget shortfall. This tactic is what economists call monetizing the debt, and is tantamount to printing money. The maneuver may relieve interest-rate pressure, at least for the moment. But it may also push money-supply growth above what Fed officials may deem a range appropriate to the economy's ability to expand. It's precisely for such reasons that the growth of the various Ms has so often exceeded rates consistent with an economy that can increase in healthy fashion at a pace of roughly 3 to 4 percent a year.

In the 1970s, when inflation was particularly troublesome, the portion of the federal deficit purchased each year by the Fed averaged 32 percent. Without this buying, the federal government would have had a tougher time borrowing in the credit market, but the money supply would have grown at less inflationary rates, at a pace more in line with the economy's natural capacity to expand.

STILL another major prescription for setting the economy right is the so-called supply-side idea. Supply-side theory, however, is in reality nothing more than the ultimate ideological expression of our extravagance, our effort to keep on living beyond our means. It's no more workable than fiscalism or monetarism. Supply-side advocates maintain that the key to sustained economic growth is cutting taxes, which, they say, will induce people to work harder, knowing that they will be able to hold on to more of their pay, and investors to invest more readily, knowing that whatever return they eventually receive won't be largely diverted to the Internal Revenue Service. The result, in the supply-side scenario, is a faster-growing, more efficient, more bountiful economy, with low joblessness, low interest rates, and low inflation. An added benefit is deemed to be that deficits in the federal budget will swiftly diminish and ultimately disappear, supposedly because a brisker economy will generate such a sharp rise in incomes that tax receipts will climb, even though rates are reduced.

It's all a wonderful-sounding notion, particularly for politicians seeking office. There's no question that it played a large role in winning President Reagan his first term. It promises the proverbial free lunch, a perfectly painless—almost magical—way in which to strengthen the economy, cut the budget deficit, and take a large step toward economic utopia.

In fact, the supply-side idea is really hokum. Reagan's first-term tax reductions began with the Economic Recovery Tax Act passed in 1981, which trimmed personal income-tax rates by a hefty 23 percent over three years, reduced the tax on two-earner families, introduced indexing of tax-bracket creep due to inflation, starting in 1985, and lowered the effective tax rates on income from saving and investment. But the budget deficit more than doubled in the wake of these tax cuts. Despite brisk economic growth in 1983 and 1984, the deficit has remained enormous, remaining well over $200 billion as late as 1986, with the economic expansion nearing its fourth birthday.

Many supply-side advocates aren't bona fide economists at all but political activists of varying stripes who managed to gain President Reagan's ear early on. Karl Brunner, who has professorships at the universities of Rochester in New York

and Bern in Switzerland, characterizes supply-side economics as a largely nonsensical concept that has emerged through
an interaction between "the media and a small group of
advocates. . . ." These include Arthur Laffer, creator of the
famous Laffer curve, an economist with political aspirations;
Jude Wanniski, a political consultant and a former *Wall
Street Journal* editorial-page writer; Paul Craig Roberts, another former *Journal* editorialist as well as a former Treasury
Department official; Robert Bartley, who is in overall charge
of the *Journal*'s editorial page; and Republican Congressman
Jack Kemp, the former professional football player who is a
close friend of Wanniski's and a contender for his party's
presidential nomination in 1988.

Around the time that the tax-cut plan was being debated,
skeptics were questioning the supply-side notion that the
federal-budget deficits posed no problem. Wanniski was
asked, Why not? His response was typical of the group's ability to dismiss doubts with catchy, glib rejoinders. "How long
does it take you," he replied, "to stoop down and grab a
ten-dollar bill you see lying on the street?"

The media outlet for the supply-side theorists was afforded
by Bartley. Through his management of the *Journal*'s editorial page, the various supply-siders were able to disseminate
their free-lunch theory to a wide, influential readership in
the nation's most widely read newspaper. Through Kemp,
the group gained White House attention. The Reagan tax
cuts followed.

Murray L. Weidenbaum, who served as chairman of President Reagan's Council of Economic Advisers when the Laff-
er-Wanniski influence was at its peak, now looks back
ruefully at the supply-siders' legislative success. Now an economics professor at Washington University in St. Louis, Weidenbaum declares: "For far too many people, supply-side
economics was the latest promise of a free lunch [and, to
make matters worse,] visions of rapidly rising revenues
dampened the ardor for budget cuts." George Will, the

columnist, put it more bluntly in a 1984 address in New York City, in which he lamented the huge budget deficit. *"The Wall Street Journal,"* he said, "has a lot to answer for."[1]

Supply-side economics provides the ultimate illustration of our national self-indulgence, the same self-indulgence that has invalidated both fiscalist and monetarist theory. Supply-side economics is nothing more than a new pretext for our extravagance.

NO theory or prescription can stand up to the kind of reality that confronts us now, after so many years of living beyond our means. And this inability is apparent even in the international arena. In the earlier postwar years, international financial dealings were conducted along Keynesian lines, under what was known as the Bretton Woods system. Designed in the latter days of World War II by Lord Keynes and others at the New Hampshire resort of Bretton Woods, the system was set up so that currency values among the major industrial countries would remain fixed in relation to one another. This was achieved by tying the dollar's own value to a set amount of gold—$35 per ounce—and then tying the value of other currencies to that of the dollar. The U.S., with a huge supply of gold at the end of World War II, stood ready supposedly to buy or sell the yellow metal in transactions with other governments at a rate of $35 per ounce. At the same time, other governments supposedly stood ready to buy or sell dollars in such a way as to maintain the agreed-upon fixed relationships between their currencies and the dollar, whose value was anchored to gold.

As things developed in practice, however, this fixed-rate system acted to insulate the U.S. economy from inflationary pressures that might otherwise have developed within the U.S. Instead, these strains were transmitted abroad. Just how this transpired can be illustrated by recalling events in West Germany in 1971, the year that the Bretton Woods system finally collapsed. On May 5 of that year, the Bundesbank, West Germany's central bank, stopped buying dollars for marks and, in essence, allowed the dollar to float downward in relation to the mark. In the forty-eight hours beforehand, however, West German officials had been forced under Bretton Woods rules to purchase more than $2 billion at the fixed dollar-mark rate of exchange, issuing marks for the American currency. Such buying, as the West German officials complained bitterly at the time, served to severely aggravate inflation in their country, by causing the West Germany money supply to rise at about twice the desired rate.

Under Bretton Woods rules, the West Germans could have sought U.S. gold at the $35-per-ounce price for the unwanted dollars piling up at the Bundesbank. In practice, however, the West Germans—like other foreign central bankers similarly inundated—were hesitant to issue such a request. It had grown increasingly evident that America's shrinking gold supply could no longer be counted on to meet the potential demands of dollar holders abroad. The inevitable outcome of this bind was the West German decision, shortly followed by similar ones elsewhere, to stop buying dollars for marks.

Since the 1971 collapse of the Bretton Woods system, an international financial arrangement has prevailed, for lack of any agreed-upon alternatives, that Professor Friedman and most other monetarists enthusiastically endorsed while the Bretton Woods system was in place. It entails, quite simply, allowing the various key currencies to float in relation to one another, in response to forces of supply and demand for the various currencies. Under current arrangements, no government is obliged to swallow unwanted dollars at a fixed rate of exchange if dollars pile up there. According to the floating-rate advocates, inflation, at least in theory, could no longer be transmitted abroad, as happened under fixed rates. Excessive dollars, they said, would henceforth—and quite properly —generate inflation at home and not abroad. If the Federal Reserve proved overly expansionary or fiscal policy overly stimulative, the dollar's worth in international markets would surely drop. This, in turn, would generate inflationary pressures in the U.S., as imports into America would grow costlier while foreign demand for cheaper U.S. exports would swell and spur business activity at home. In a world of floating exchange rates, Milton Friedman predicted before they were a fact, the U.S. government would no longer be able to pursue inflationary policies with impunity. He charged that the Bretton Woods system, in sorry contrast, allowed "inflationary policies to be disguised."

The reality of how effectively a floating-rate arrangement works grew painfully apparent in the mid-1980s, a decade and a half after the abandonment of fixed rates. At mid-decade, the U.S. had the deepest trade deficit in its history, far exceeding $100 billion yearly, as imports increasingly overwhelmed exports. And yet the dollar's international value was relatively strong, causing the trade imbalance to progressively worsen in a sort of vicious circle that could only end in, among other things, farm bankruptcies. In early 1985, the dollar's worth in terms of the British pound, to cite just one case, was at an all-time high. But this strength hardly reflected any U.S. policy of belt-tightening or parsimony at the Federal Reserve. Rising red ink suffused the federal budget, and the money supply kept rising faster than the economy's long-run potential. If the Bretton Woods system had allowed U.S. officials to conduct economic policy in an irresponsible, inflationary fashion, as Professor Friedman charged, so, apparently, does the floating-rate arrangement, endorsed by the monetarists, that has succeeded it.

Surveying the economic landscape in 1983, Felix Rohatyn, a senior partner at the investment-banking house of Lazard Frères & Co., remarked that "people are not only becoming more skeptical of economic theory, but it is highly appropriate that they do so." Unfortunately, Rohatyn himself offered no new remedies, but only a rehash of the sort of central-planning concepts questioned by Professor Hayek.

In September 1984, Francis H. Schott, the chief economist of the Equitable Life Assurance Society of the United States, was honored by the New York Association of Business Economists for his outstanding record as a forecaster and as a leader within his profession. Responding to the honor, the bespectacled economist told his audience: "Whatever success I've had I ascribe at least partly to my firm resistance . . . to the popular theories of Keynesians, monetarists, and the supply-siders."

The final word on the value of economists and their ideas belongs, perhaps, to the executives of New York's Chemical Bank. In August 1985, they decided that they could manage perfectly well, thank you, without any economics department at all. Chemical's economics staff of forty was promptly disbanded. Alan Greenspan, himself a noted economic consultant who served as President Ford's top economic adviser, calls the move a sign that "there is a vague disillusionment with economists; we are not going out of style, but we are retrenching from what had been an unrealistic position about what we could accomplish." To put it bluntly, a painless solution to today's predicament is beyond the means of any economic theory.

Chapter 5

The Enduring Cycle

To observe that nothing seems to work, that no theory of managing the economy appears practicable, isn't to say that the economy has entered completely uncharted waters. At least one constant endures, and this is the business cycle. It serves as a useful guide in assessing the economy's prospects, in the long run as well as the short. But what, precisely, do we mean by the business cycle? What are its causes? Is it inevitable? What are its ramifications? Can its progress be anticipated with a reasonable degree of accuracy?

A cycle, as Mr. Webster explains, comprises a series of developments that tend to repeat themselves over and over in the same chronological order. The repetition isn't necessarily exact with each cyclical phase, but it's close enough. The type of cycle that economists have in mind is distinguished by a sequence of well-recognized phases. First, there's a so-called business-cycle trough, when overall business reaches a cyclical low point. The yardstick normally applied is what economists call the real GNP, or the gross national product adjusted for price change; it's the broadest available measure of general economic activity. The precise month in which a trough occurs is determined by a panel of economists, the business-cycle dating group of the nonprofit National Bureau of Economic Research. For example, the group set November 1982 as the trough month of the long 1981–82 recession. The determination was made many months after the fact, when all the key numbers were in from Washington's statistics mills and had been carefully assessed.

A business-cycle trough month, besides marking the pit of a recession, also denotes the start of an expansionary phase of the cycle. Thus, November 1982 marks both the bottom of the 1981–82 recession and the start of the subsequent economic upswing. The business-cycle dating group doesn't cut things so finely, but strictly speaking, the first half of November 1982 qualifies as a part of the 1981–82 recession and the second half of the month as the beginning of the ensuing economic expansion (which was the result, as we have seen, of the Fed's highly stimulative monetary policy in 1982).

An expansionary phase of the cycle is normally characterized by progressive increases in the real GNP, along with such other beneficial developments as rising profits, increasing factory production, climbing employment, and shrinking joblessness. Expansions finally end with a business-cycle peak, when real GNP and the other main barometers of business activity typically are at record levels and about to start falling. The dating group placed the peak preceding the 1981–82 recession in July 1981. Thus, the first half of that month is regarded as part of the 1980–81 expansion, an extraordinarily short upturn of the cycle, and the second half of the month marked the onset of the 1981–82 recession, which, most unusually, was several months longer than the preceding expansion.

These ups and downs of the business cycle—trough, ensuing expansion, peak, ensuing recession or, as economists call it, contraction—have been tracked by National Bureau analysts all the way back to 1854, more exactly to December of that year, deemed a trough month in the record book. Since then, the research organization, using a variety of economic statistics including GNP data, has recorded thirty expansions, through the 1980–81 upswing, and thirty contractions, through the 1981–82 slump.[1]

The up phases, fortunately, have been a good deal longer, on the average, than the down phases. Indeed, this is how the economy has grown over the decades, in a sort of two-steps-forward, one-step-back fashion. The expansions, trough to peak, work out to an average duration of 33 months. The contractions, peak to trough, average 18 months. The longest of the expansions occurred in 1961–69, lasting 106 months, and the shortest ran from the spring of 1919 to early 1920, only 10 months. The longest contraction happened all the way back in 1873–79 and spanned 65 months. The shortest took place relatively recently, in early 1980, and lasted only 6 months.

National Bureau analysts have subdivided their business-cycle data into three narrower time frames—from 1854 to 1919, an interval encompassing sixteen ups and downs of the cycle; from 1919 to 1945, which spans six cyclical ups and downs; and from 1945 onward, a period encompassing eleven cycles up to the expansion that exactly coincided with Ronald Reagan's first presidential election victory in November 1980.

Viewed along chronological lines, this breakdown points up some notable patterns. Expansions have been growing progressively longer. In the 1854–1919 stretch, the cyclical upturns averaged 27 months. In 1919–45, the average increased to 35 months. And in the latest period, it reached 45 months, a full year and a half longer than in the pre-World War I decades. Recessions, by the same token, have been slowly shrinking in length. In 1854–1919, contraction phases of the cycle averaged 22 months; in 1919–45, 18 months; and in 1945-onward, only 11 months.

By and large, the longest expansion periods have coincided partly or wholly with wars. The long 1961–69 upturn roughly coincided with the Vietnam War. The second-longest expansion was also largely a wartime affair, the eighty-month upswing of 1938–45. At the same time, the longest contractions have tended to occur in peacetime. The long 1873–79 slump is an example. Better known and more painful was the forty-three-month downturn of 1929–1933. Its March 1933 trough is generally viewed as the Great Depression's low point.

Sturdy, long-running expansions often follow in the wake of severe recessions. By the same token, weak, short-lived upturns often occur after short, mild recessions. The longest peacetime expansion, a fifty-eight-month upswing from early 1975 until the start of 1980, followed one of the most severe recessions of the postwar era, the sixteen-month slump of 1973–75. The weak upturn of 1980–81, the shortest on record after the 1919–20 expansion, followed on the heels of the record-short six-month recession of 1980.

NONE of these patterns is happenstance. Enduring expansions naturally tend to follow severe recessions because such slumps act to cleanse the economy of the strains and distortions that normally mark a peak in the business cycle. These range from intense inflationary pressures to climbing interest rates to shortages of material and labor to bottlenecks in production and delivery schedules. In similar fashion, weak expansions tend to follow mild recessions precisely because such recessions fail to provide the necessary cleaning out. They fail to lay the groundwork for renewed, vigorous economic growth. In such circumstances, inflation and other boom-time problems rapidly reemerge as business activity begins to move up from the business-cycle trough. As these problems intensify, further economic gains grow increasingly difficult. The upshot: a subpar, abbreviated expansion.

The tendency of expansions to lengthen and recessions to shorten in recent decades isn't happenstance, either. Particularly since World War II, as noted earlier, transfer payments have acted to blunt recessions. Ever more generous programs of unemployment relief have served to shore up consumer buying power even as joblessness has spread. Thanks to transfer payments, consumer spending kept right on rising through the otherwise severe recession of 1981–82, the first postwar slump in which the jobless rate reached double-digit range. As recessions have shortened, so, naturally, have expansions grown longer. As business activity has moved up from troughs, the rise in transfer income has slowed but by no means halted. Superimposed on reviving activity within the economy's private sector, this climb in transfers has further spurred expansion.

Nor is it coincidental that the most enduring upturns have tended to occur in wartime and the longest contractions in peacetime. Like transfer payments, military spending tends to pump up consumers' purchasing power—albeit in a highly inflationary manner since, as we've observed, bomb factories do nothing to enlarge the supply of goods or services available for purchase in the marketplace. When military outlays are on the increase, as during the long 1961–69 expansion, this boost to buying power serves as a powerful economic stimulant. And the effect is directly opposite when such outlays diminish. After spending for the Vietnam War began to diminish, the economy sustained two recessions, both relatively severe, within a short five years.

THESE various patterns, as important as they may be, hardly explain why a business cycle exists in the first place or why the economy, over so many decades, has shown this tendency to expand-contract, expand-contract. Why, in brief, is the business cycle, like death and taxes, always with us?

Perhaps the simplest and best explanation that I've encountered wasn't in any economic textbook but in a letter from a *Wall Street Journal* reader named Russell M. Fowler. Responding to an article that I wrote in November 1984 on the business cycle's remarkable durability, Fowler, who serves as the administrator of the Wayne Economic Development Corporation in Lyons, New York, put it this way:

> Maybe the reason the business cycle endures is the economy is solidly based on human nature. When things are going good, some human reactions occur: overconfi-

dence, complacency, poor workmanship, greed, overexpansion, mistakes; all bad and leading to [a] downturn. Then when things are going bad, there is a tendency to shape up and turn things around. Maybe that's all there is to it.

Amen. It's as clear and accurate an explanation of the why of the cycle as I've encountered, and as a description of the national mood during the upswing of 1985–86, it could hardly be better. It's good deal clearer, in fact, than anything I've managed to extract over the years from an array of eminent economists and businessmen who should know better. I've even heard eminent economists profess—though not recently—that the cycle, while it may have existed once upon a time, has been eliminated by adroit policy-making in Washington.

One such one-time believer was the late Otto Eckstein, an economic adviser to President Johnson. Professor Eckstein was fortunate enough to fill that role just when the longest upswing in business-cycle history was in progress. Before his untimely death in 1984, the Harvard economist, who also headed the highly successful economic-consulting firm of Data Resources Inc., had become convinced of the cycle's inevitability. But back in the mid-1960s, he was among the brave new economists who sincerely supposed that they could guide business activity comfortably along a path-without-end of recession-free expansion. Fine-tuning the economy was the catchword.

This conviction occasionally was stretched to ludicrous extremes, as when Eckstein and his colleagues in Washington decided that the name of the Commerce Department's premier statistical publication was no longer appropriate. The monthly publication had been called for years *Business Cycle Developments,* a to-the-point appellation in that the periodical not only reported all sorts of business data, but took the extra step of relating the various numbers back over the

decades to the ups and downs of the business cycle. The title
—in accordance with the prevailing notion that the cycle had
been eliminated forever through more enlightened policy-
making—was ordered changed to *Business Conditions Digest.* Notwithstanding the change, the economy, as perverse
as ever, soon entered a particularly nasty slump. So much for
new eras of recession-free growth. The new name has stuck,
with only the *BCD* acronym unchanged. The business cycle
has stuck as well.

As Russell Fowler indicates, contractions of business activity occur, and will continue to do so, because of an immutable
constant—human nature. Planners, be they public or private, make mistakes. When things are going along in fine
fashion, planners tend to neglect the sometimes painful belt-
tightening that in the long term might help to keep business
on the upswing. They tend to overestimate prospects for
further economic gains, inventories begin to pile up, workers
finally must be furloughed, and an expansion transforms into
a recession. And when it's all too evident that the economy
is finally on the skids, planners begin believing that the depressed conditions will keep worsening. Inventories are
worked down—perhaps too far down. Eventually, customer
demand for goods and services begins to outstrip supply.
Businesses scramble to catch up, production is stepped up,
and the economy starts recovering once again.

This recurring tendency to overestimate and underestimate will subside as soon as human nature changes, and no
sooner. It's particularly pronounced in economies, such as
the major industrial ones, where manufacturing plays a
prominent role. Manufacturing, of course, spans such important industries as automobiles, appliances, and heavy machinery, plus sundry lesser businesses. Such products must be
fashioned in factories, using such basic materials as steel,
copper, coal, aluminum, and plastics, and then be distributed
and sold to customers at home and abroad. If factory operations are precisely geared to demand, so as not to over-

produce or underproduce particular items, the economy generally should prosper and expand without nasty surprises. After all, the U.S. population continues to grow, though somewhat more slowly than in decades past. Moreover, technological advances keep coming that enhance the nation's productive efficiency; this, too, serves to prolong economic expansion.

It should be added that outside factors, as well as the fallibility of planners in and out of Washington, occasionally contribute to the economy's cyclical behavior. An example is the oil squeeze that the Arab countries imposed on the U.S. and other major oil-using countries in late 1973. It is generally agreed that the U.S. economy was still in an expansion mode, which started in 1970, when the oil squeeze developed. How much longer that expansion phase would have lasted had the Arabs not cut the oil supply is a matter of conjecture. To be sure, forces were already developing in the fall of 1973—for instance, an excessive accumulation of inventories in many businesses—that would certainly have led sooner or later to an expansion peak and a subsequent contraction of the cycle. But there seems little doubt that the jolting reduction in Middle Eastern oil supplies, with the long lines at gasoline stations and the occasional restriction of output at fuel-starved factories, hastened and deepened the new slump.

If the business cycle is inevitable, as experience and common sense suggest, what does this portend for the economy? Are we simply to sit back and suffer through the inevitable down phases of the cycle, with their spreading joblessness and sinking profits, and hope that recovery time won't prove too far over the horizon? Or should we strive to minimize, perhaps even eliminate, the contraction periods and perpetuate the expansions?

The latter course, not surprisingly, has long been a primary goal of Washington's policy-makers. The record of recent decades is marked by a succession of noble efforts to bring incipient recessions to a rapid end and, in the familiar phrase,

get the economy moving again. The main engine of this
economic stimulation has been the Federal Reserve Board
which, through its Open Market Committee, has repeatedly
moved, when the outlook seemed dark, to spur monetary
growth far faster than the economy's own long-term ability
to advance. A second source of stimulation has been the
government's proclivity, thanks mainly to the Congress, to
spend far more each year than is taken in by the tax man.
Whatever else can be said about the resulting budgetary
deficits, they have acted on balance to spur business activity.
If nothing else, federal outlays tend, at least in the shorter
term, to create jobs and spur demand for all sorts of goods
and services, and there can be no doubt that monetary and
fiscal stimulation has helped prolong expansions and limit
contractions.

So far, this stimulation has worked reasonably well, with
the upturns lengthening and the recessions, until recently,
becoming milder and shorter. But in this forced-draft effort
to alter the economy's natural patterns—its tendency to
slump, cleanse itself, and recover with renewed vigor—a
rigidity has developed that transcends the business cycle.
With each new up-and-down of the cycle, as the postwar
decades have passed, a degree of natural resiliency has
drained from the economy.

With this increasing brittleness, the business cycle takes on
a dangerous new aspect. With each new contraction phase,
the possibility of a real collapse grows larger. Because we
have lived so far beyond our means for so long, the economy
has come to require ever greater doses of adrenaline to recover. The doses, to be sure, have been quickly supplied in
massive quantity—as when the Federal Reserve explosively
expanded the money supply in 1982, and the feared collapse
hasn't materialized. But the treatment gets riskier and trickier the longer it's applied. In brief, the decades-long effort to
modify the business cycle has led to the crisis of institutions
that now confronts us.

With the brittleness, the expansions also require more attention. Unemployment proves stickier, generally settling in at higher and higher levels with each new business-cycle peak. Corporate balance sheets stay shakier for longer. The rate of bankruptcies subsides less readily. Inflationary dislocations—shortages, delivery delays, labor-cost increases, stagnant productivity, price increases—tend to redevelop at lower and lower levels of capacity utilization. In the process, the economy requires larger and larger doses of medication to avert a relapse. These have been amply applied by the various successions of authorities in Washington, be they Republican or Democrat. But again, the game grows trickier.

A few statistics help to illustrate the general pattern. Near the trough of the 1981–82 recession, the unemployment rate was about 11 percent, compared to 9 percent near the trough of the severe 1973–75 slump and only about 6 percent near the trough of the 1969–70 recession. There has been a similar worsening in the amount of current liabilities outstanding from business failures. During the 1981–82 recession, the total reached a monthly rate of some $1.8 billion, up from about $350 million in 1973–75 and just under $200 million in 1969–70.

If only the business cycle could be made to fade away, but this eventuality is as likely as an overnight transformation of New York City's subway system into the safest, cleanest mass-transit operation in the world. It's not about to happen. And so the danger mounts that with each new contraction of the cycle an increasingly brittle economy will crack, and not simply creak and groan once again in another of the string of postwar recessions.

Fiscal and monetary stimulation implemented to prolong expansions and shorten recessions works in essence like a drug, masking symptoms that should be attended to directly. The economic system never gets cleansed during recessions of excesses—for example, excessive borrowing—that accumulated during periods of general economic growth. In

the process, larger and larger doses of stimulation are necessary to induce a given amount of growth. Example: Despite
repeated income-tax cuts, more liberal tax treatment of corporate investments, and an exceptionally swift rise in the
money supply during the early Reagan years, overall economic growth was largely subpar for an expansion period,
averaging only 3 percent or less annually through much of
the time.

BEFORE moving on from the business cycle, it may be useful
to examine briefly how the cycle's future ups and downs may
be anticipated with a reasonable degree of accuracy. There's
no magic to the procedure, only a need to be familiar with
a limited variety of statistical barometers, readily available,
that tend faithfully to presage the cycle's near-term progress.

Far and away the most highly publicized and widely monitored of these barometers is a measure produced monthly by
economists at the Commerce Department. Called the composite index of leading indicators, it comprises a dozen statistical barometers, which range from the length of the average
work week for production workers to the broadly defined M2
version of the money supply, expressed in so-called constant
dollars to eliminate "growth" reflecting merely inflation.
Other components include the stock market, as reflected in
the five hundred-common-stock index of Standard & Poor's
Corp.; vendor performance, a measure of the speed with
which materials are delivered; an index of the rate at which
new businesses are being formed; a measure of unemploy-
ment-insurance claims; a yardstick showing monthly changes
in outstanding business and consumer debt; a composite
price index for various raw materials found to be especially
sensitive to shifts in supply-and-demand pressures; a measure
of inventory change at various levels of business transaction;
the volume of new-home permits; a gauge of new orders for

consumer goods; and the volume of contracts and new orders for plant and equipment. Those barometers expressed in dollar terms are adjusted monthly by the Commerce statisticians, as in the case of M2, to eliminate any movements reflecting merely price change.

The leading-indicator composite, which was developed in the early post-World War II era, has foreshadowed the economy's ups and downs with impressive regularity over many years. On the average, it has entered a sustained decline some ten months before the arrival of a business-cycle peak. It has never failed to give some warning that a contraction was on the way, though the lead-time has varied greatly— from only three months before the 1981–82 recession to twenty-three months before the 1957–58 slump. Since the indicator tends to bounce around from month to month, economic forecasters generally hold that a sustained decline isn't under way unless there has been a drop extending over at least three months.

The composite index is somewhat less useful in helping forecasters anticipate a business-cycle trough. Normally, its lead-time in a recession is far shorter than in an expansion; recessions tend to end more abruptly than cyclical upswings, and of course they are generally much shorter. On the average, the indicator has signaled troughs by just over three months. It has never failed to give some advanced signal, but twice, the lead-time was only a month. The earliest signal, before the trough of the 1981–82 contraction, was eight months.

The Commerce Department's composite, it should be noted, is but one of many statistical barometers that economic forecasters use to try to keep a step or two ahead of the business cycle's fluctuations. Its great advantage is its ready availability. Commerce analysts release the report to the press on a monthly basis, usually within a couple of days of a month's end, and it's generally picked up on radio and television news programs that day and given prominent display a day later in such newspapers as *The Wall Street Journal* and *The New York Times*. With each new turn of the business cycle, one or another of the dozen components may behave misleadingly. By trusting a composite of so many barometers, forecasters minimize the chance of being misled by a single strange-behaving statistic.

A case in point is the behavior of the stock-market indicator before the 1980 recession. In a study of the various indicators, analysts at the National Bureau of Economic Research have determined that the stock market, as reflected in the monthly average of the Standard & Poor's share-price gauge, has served over the postwar years as the very best of the key barometers of what's ahead for business. The assessment is based on such criteria as timeliness and reliability. Out of a possible rating of 100, the market indicator received 85; the next highest score for any of the other eleven components was 80, assigned to the vendor-performance measure.

For all its reliability, however, the market indicator utterly failed to foreshadow the 1980 recession. In January 1980, when the economy once again began to nose down into a recession, the stock-market gauge was still on the rise. There was no signal that a slump was imminent—unless one takes the trouble to adjust the indicator for inflation. As noted, all dollar-denominated components of the Commerce Department's composite are inflation-adjusted. But strictly speaking, the share-price measure isn't expressed in dollars, even though the underlying individual share prices of the five hundred stocks are, of course, stated in dollar terms. When an adjustment is made, the market barometer turns out to have been in a long decline in January 1980, dating from the fall of 1976. That amounts to a recession warning of forty months.

While the Commerce Department still doesn't adjust share prices for inflation, it's a simple procedure to do it

yourself. Let's assume, for example, that the share-price measure, as released by the Commerce Department, rises 2 percent in a given month and that the consumer price index in
the same period climbs 1 percent. In such a situation, the
inflation-adjusted gain in the market indicator would be only
1 percent, or half as large as officially reported.

A footnote on the 1980 recession: While the stock-market
measure, distorted by inflation, gave no warning that a cyclical peak was at hand, the Commerce Department's twelve-
indicator composite entered a sustained decline fully ten
months before the 1980 recession finally arrived. The lesson:
Business-cycle forecasters should watch a variety of leading
indicators, no matter how highly rated a particular barometer may be.

This isn't to imply that anyone trying to keep ahead of the
business cycle should disregard the behavior of individual
barometers. The inflation-adjusted money supply, for instance, has rarely emitted false signals and has generally
warned of recessions extra early. It has correctly signaled
every recession since the 1969–70 slump—four in all—and
the warning times have ranged from about six months to as
long as two years, before the 1980 recession.

The difficulty is that unlike stock-market prices, the M2
barometer receives relatively little publicity. If it lands in the
newspaper columns at all, it usually is tucked away in the fine
print near the bottom of the monthly Commerce Department report on the composite index. More often than not,
the monetary measure doesn't even make the fine print. It's
compiled, of course, by the Federal Reserve Board, but unfortunately, the Fed doesn't bother to make any adjustment
for inflation; that task is left to Commerce near month's end,
when the department is readying its leading-indicator report.

Another good indicator, not a part of the Commerce composite, is the Dow Jones corporate-bond index. Far less fa-

mous that the thirty-stock Dow Jones Industrial Average, the bond index reflects price changes in twenty bellweather bond issues. Like the stock index, however, the bond measure is reported daily in *The Wall Street Journal,* atop the paper's listing for corporate-bond trading on the New York exchange. Over many decades, the bond-price index, taken as a monthly average, has given particularly early, reliable indications of where general business activity may move next. It has been especially early in signaling the approach of a business-cycle trough. This is useful to forecasters because, as we have seen, the Commerce composite often provides only a month or two of lead-time at such points in the cycle. It's noteworthy that in mid-1985, when some forecasters, concerned about the slow pace of economic growth, were speculating that another recession was developing, the bond index was climbing steadily, a strong sign that the economic course was likelier to continue upward, which in fact turned out to be the situation.

Keeping ahead of the cycle, then, is not an impossible chore.[2] Through careful, regular scrutiny of the various leading indicators, it's possible to glimpse with remarkable accuracy how, in very broad terms, the economy is likely to perform several months down the road. No one watching the leading-indicator index should have been surprised, for example, that a business-cycle trough occurred in November 1982, since the composite indicator had been climbing steadily for eight months.

After so many years of living beyond our means, however, it's no longer sufficient simply to monitor the business cycle and, using the various early-warning barometers, try to anticipate when the next twist or turn will come in the economic road. As suggested earlier, a new brittleness has set in during the post-World War II decades that now pervades the economic structure. The business cycle surely will persist, but ominous longer-term forces are also at work. Human nature underlies the persistence of the business cycle. But its influence on the economy's performance, as we'll see, goes even deeper than that.

BEFORE leaving the matter of the business cycle, I should note that it's by no means the only sort of cycle that some economists perceive, though it's the only one that, in my view, makes sense. By and large, the others appear to be figments of the imagination of their various sponsors and, I would stress, should never be confused with the business cycle, as described above and defined by the National Bureau of Economic Research.

Perhaps the best known of these other, dubious, cycles is the so-called Kondratieff Wave, named for Nicolai Dimitrievich Kondratieff, a Russian economist who undertook his main research in the 1920s. Kondratieff became convinced that a business super-cycle runs through economic history, in a relentless pattern of depression, revival, and uncertainty before depression-time once again rolls around. His theory rests in large measure on what he determined to be long-term cyclical patterns in a number of key commodity prices in the major industrial nations. In the U.S., for instance, Kondratieff wholesale-price peaks are apparent around the War of 1812, about a half century later at the time of Civil War and, moving forward another half century, around the time of World War I.

Drawing from such price patterns, the Russian suggested that general business activity in the capitalist West—his research focused mainly on the U.S., Britain, and France—exhibits a regular wavelike pattern over extremely long periods.[3] At its heart, Kondratieff theory holds that every half century or so, economies break down for a variety of reasons ranging from insufficient demand to inappropriate investment to, quite simply, human nature—a new generation repeating, in different form, the policy mistakes of its predecessor.

There's an ironic footnote. One would suppose that a Soviet economist who devised a theory predicting, in effect,
that Western economies would collapse every fifty years or
so would earn high praise from the Soviet government. Instead, he was banished by Stalin to Siberia, where he was
assigned to the salt mines until he finally died. Today his
name is virtually unknown inside Russia, but his brutal fate
is recorded in *The Gulag Archipelago*, by Alexander I.
Solzhenitsyn. According to *The Gulag*, the economist
finished his days in "solitary confinement" in Siberia, "became mentally ill . . . and died."

The reason he was banished rather than rewarded for his
theory was that in essence, it held out the promise of re-
demption for capitalism, for while depressions would come
roughly every half century, so would recoveries. Kondratieff
foresaw that a process of economic renewal was at work
during these periodic capitalistic slumps. He also theorized
that out of this would ultimately come vigorous new prosperity. This wasn't the sort of message that Stalin or his Marxist
colleagues welcomed.

A December 1984 study by a group of Montreal economists
contained in *The Bank Credit Analyst* casts doubt, however,
on whether a clearly definable long wave really exists. First,
it contends that Kondratieff's statistical techniques were
"seriously flawed" by his "arbitrary starting points in calcu-
lating the all-important trend" of prices. Second, it maintains
that evidence of economic "hard times" to coincide with the
fifty-year pattern is mainly apparent only in wage-and-price
data, while industrial production seems actually to have risen
in some of the periods designated by Kondratieff as depressions. The Great Depression was the exception rather than
the rule.

The Montreal study further states that "Kondratieff's empirical evidence is open to serious question. . . . Using modern
techniques, there is no evidence of the long wave in Kondratieff's own data." The study adds that "extending the data

. . . both forward and back in time, provides no evidence of the long wave," even though this may be "rather difficult to stomach for those who have always assumed the validity of the long wave."

While they deny any precise Kondratieff cycle—"the vision of man bound to a large slow-turning wheel, unable to avoid having his head dunked in the mire at regular intervals"—the Montreal economists do caution that longer repetitive patterns, transcending the familiar business cycle, may well be at work. They concede that "economic processes are by nature cyclical" and that "all periods of inflation are [eventually] followed by deflation, and the deflationary process begins when the anticipation of continued inflation is widely accepted as inevitable."

Whatever the validity of the Kondratieff Wave theory, an important point is, once again, that economic developments are deeply rooted in human nature. People tend to overextend themselves, given the opportunity. Banks invariably will run down liquidity by bidding more and more aggressively for deposits, accepting lower-quality credits, and shaving loan charges. Corporations invariably will overexpand if they think they can accelerate earnings growth and gain a larger market share. Politicians invariably will mortgage more and more of the future in order to promise voters more today. And as a nation, we will invariably tend to discount future income by borrowing larger and larger amounts in order to live better now. But as these debts mount, so does the cost of servicing them, and individuals, companies, and even the federal government become less able to absorb the unexpected economic shocks that reduce income below anticipated levels.

A nineteenth-century French economist, Clement Juglar, an early long-wave proponent—there's even a Juglar cycle named for him—succinctly summarized why, in his view, long waves exist. "The cause of depression," he wrote, quite simply "is prosperity." A prominent modern-day believer is

Julian M. Snyder, who has published an English translation of Kondratieff's work. Snyder, who publishes a widely followed investment letter titled *International Moneyline,* feels that the Kondratieff cycle is very much alive and that there are "ominous warnings" that a long-wave downturn is at hand. Among the signs, he says, are rising real-estate vacancy rates, sagging farm incomes, proliferating bank failures, and sharply climbing home-mortgage delinquencies and foreclosures. Sharing the Snyder view is a leading Dutch analyst, Jakob van Duijin, who declares: "Long-wave theories are becoming popular because they fit what we see is happening."

IF the economy is indeed guided by long as well as shorter cyclical patterns, then the bulk of the post-World War II era seems unmistakably to constitute a long-wave upswing. In the long-wave concept, as the economy slowly builds toward a super-cycle peak, familiar patterns become pronounced. Capital investment plays a diminishing role in overall economic activity. Unemployment tends to stick at higher and higher levels. Productivity advances prove harder to achieve. Interest rates tend at each short-cycle peak to level off at higher and higher readings. Inflation follows a similar pattern. The income return to investors falls faster during contractions and rises less briskly when business activity picks up again.

Not all proponents of the long-wave idea agree that the wave runs for about fifty years. Among other waves named for their particular sponsors, for example, is the so-called Kuznets cycle, whose length ranges from fifteen to twenty years. It was conceived by Simon Kuznets, a Nobel-laureate economist who taught at Harvard for many years and pioneered in establishing statistical ways to measure overall economic activity. Barely half as long as the Kondratieff cycle, the Kuznets cycle hinges on periodic swings in construction activity; particular attention is paid as well to broad population trends.

And the list goes on. Some analysts cite an eighteen-year real-estate cycle, a nine-year financial cycle, a six-year gold cycle, and a four-year stock-market cycle. However many more cycles various economists may claim to observe, Antal E. Fekete, a mathematics professor at the Memorial University of Newfoundland, stresses that "the study of cycles is not an exact science" but rather "is strictly empirical." Accordingly, he urges that cyclical theories not be given undue emphasis in efforts to assess the economy's prospects. Similarly, Sir Arthur Lewis, a Nobel laureate in economics at Princeton University, several years ago said that he's convinced that "long periods of relative prosperity" tend to alternate with "long periods of relative stagnation." He added that "if you ask if I believe in . . . long waves, the answer is: probably yes." But he didn't detect any precision to it, in the sense of a regularly occurring fifty-year super-cycle. He sensed, at the most, a variety of "longish cycles." Among the possibilities that he cited are an approximate fifty-year cycle, which "we really don't have the evidence to support, and an eighteen-to-twenty year construction cycle, which gives ten years of prosperity and ten years of stagnation."

The prudent course may be to recognize that long-term as well as short-term patterns play a crucial role in how the economy behaves. Unlike the shorter cycle that the National Bureau analysts track, longer cycles aren't readily reflected in one or another of the economic indicators produced in Washington. There's no Commerce Department index of leading economic indicators available to warn forecasters that within several months or so, a long-wave peak on the order, say, of August 1929 will arrive. Nor, by the same token, is there any barometer to signal when a sustained economic upswing—as happened after the long-wave trough of the Great Depression—is on the way.

While the economy's longer-run patterns can't be gauged

precisely, it's still possible to sense the general drift—
whether, by Kondratieff standards, things seem to be on the
upswing or the downswing or possibly at a long-wave turning
point. If the evidence points toward a turning point from a
long-wave upswing to a downswing, it isn't difficult to recognize that hard times may lie ahead. The economy will continue to have its business-cycle expansions and contractions,
but the former will prove disappointingly lackluster and the
latter unexpectedly severe.

This is precisely what the outlook seems to hold at present.
And it matters little whether a long-wave downswing is to
blame or—more realistically, in my view—the postwar habit
of living beyond our means. The central point is that the
economy's prospects appear severely limited, as we will see,
by what has gone before, by our own extravagant behavior
throughout the postwar era.

Chapter 6

Spending Rolls On

There's an obvious solution to the problem of having lived too long beyond one's means, and it applies to nations as well as individuals. It's to spend less, save more, and work harder. Individuals, of course, can occasionally enjoy a windfall, such as an inheritance from a rich uncle. But nations, at least big, powerful ones like the U.S., have no such benefactors and no choice in the long run but to tighten the belt and mend spendthrift ways.

But this requires, with nations as with individuals, a considerable amount of fortitude. And in the long range of history, it is hard to think of a nation that has lived consistently beyond its means and then mended its ways and regained a previous vigor. It is all too easy to think of countries—Britain and Argentina spring to mind—that have lived beyond their means and fallen into decline.

Can the U.S. begin to live within its means, which is to say, can we cut the budget deficit, grow more productive, and compete more efficiently in world markets? Does the national will exist to achieve this? So far, there is little if any evidence that it does.

If ever in the postwar era there has been an administration equipped ideologically to cut expenditures, it's that of Ronald Reagan. Yet under Reagan, as we have seen, deficits have grown and grown and remained at enormous levels at a point in the upswing of the business cycle when the red ink normally is minimal. In 1980, President Carter's last full year in office, the federal government spent $577 billion, a very large sum, but puny alongside the $842 billion that the government spent in 1984, the last year of Reagan's first term. In the first four years of Reagan "austerity," the nation's annual budgetary outlays rose by $265 billion, or 45 percent. The increase alone almost equals the federal government's total outlays in 1974, a decade earlier.

This reality belies the notion, fostered by misleading press coverage, that stringent measures have cut a variety of federal programs to the bone. In the single month of February 1985, for instance, a headline in *The Washington Post* proclaimed, "20 Million Found to Go Hungry"; one in *The Honolulu Advertiser* stated, "Survey Finds Surprisingly Low Health-Care Coverage in U.S."; and one in the New York *Daily News* blared, "Ron's Budget Ax Whacks N.Y.; Layoffs, Fare Hikes Feared."

This impression of a federal frugality is simply false, and to understand how the spending and big deficits keep rolling on, let's examine how the federal budget breaks down. In 1985, for example, 48 percent of all federal spending was for "human resources"—a broad category embracing, among other things, education, health, and welfare services, Social Security, veterans' benefits, job training, and unemployment compensation. The next largest category was defense, which consumed nearly 26 percent of the budget. Next was a category called interest on various federal borrowings, which consumed about 13 percent of the total. A category labeled physical resources accounted for most of the remaining 14 percent of the spending; it includes such diverse components as energy, environmental protection, transportation, and regional development.

It's apparent in this breakdown that much of the budget is beyond President Reagan's control, or for that matter anyone's control. For example, interest outlays, which rose by 88.5 percent in the 1980–85 period, are virtually immune to legislative restraint and can be reined in only if interest rates fall and stay down and if a substantial share of the national debt is reduced. But this would require not merely a reduction in the annual deficits, but actual surpluses, a prospect about a likely as Rodney Dangerfield's winning a prize as the most admired man of the year. In other words, 13 percent of the budget, under present circumstances, simply cannot be trimmed.

Another very large component of the budget that rose sharply in 1980–85—nearly 44 percent, after adjusting for inflation—is defense. This is no surprise, since Reagan repeatedly has stressed that in the Carter years, and even earlier under past Republican administrations, the nation's military posture was allowed to weaken dangerously. Reagan plugged hard in his first term to boost defense spending, but finally in 1985 the president agreed to freeze—at least in inflation-adjusted terms—further yearly defense increases. The concession was widely seen as a major White House move to win popular support for additional spending restraint in other, more popular areas, but it hardly could be regarded as a legitimate step in the direction of belt-tightening, for defense cutbacks normally have little immediate impact on the general public. Moreover, it's far less painful for a politician to vote against a new weapons program than to endorse, say, a freeze in Social Security pay increases.

When Reagan agreed to freeze such spending, Pentagon buying amounted to just under 7 percent of gross national product, up from about 5 percent in early 1981, when he first took office. But the 1985 rate remained substantially below the 8 percent-plus levels that prevailed through much of the 1950s and 1960s. By past standards, then, the nation had hardly become an armed camp as a result of the early Reagan effort to beef up our military strength.

Reagan adopted this freeze even though U.S.-Soviet relations remained tense, Central America and the Middle East were still unsettled, and a Reagan-Gorbachev summit meeting was not yet in prospect. Yet faced with an economic need to hold down spending, the Washington leadership seized on defense as the place to rein it in. At the time, the economist Herbert Stein, who served years earlier as President Nixon's chief economic adviser, remarked in *The Wall Street Journal* that "somebody has to tell the American people there are costs to the survival of a free society on a small planet." I agree entirely. Cutting back on defense is a dubious route to the sound economic goal of a budget more nearly in balance. "If taxes are raised, about 200 million people know that they have been hurt, and if social programs are cut, at least 50 million people know they have been hurt," Stein noted, adding, "Who knows, or will know, that he has been hurt if the defense program is cut—until it is too late?"[1]

There's an additional point. Waste permeates the military establishment, to be sure. Reports of the Pentagon paying, for example, $400 for a toilet seat are plentiful. But any implication that such extravagance is somehow unique within the military is wrong. Waste is inevitable within any huge organization, whether in the governmental or private sector. The larger the enterprise, the likelier is wastefulness, and no private organization is as enormous as the military. The military is likelier to buy $400 toilet seats than General Motors, which not only is smaller but strives to earn a profit. But General Motors is likelier to buy them than is *The Wall Street Journal*, which is smaller still.

As for the notion occasionally expressed that military personnel themselves are often slothful and should somehow be spurred to greater productivity, let me recount a personal observation. For some of the Reagan years, my oldest son served as the supply officer on the USS *San Francisco*, a nuclear-powered submarine based in Hawaii. His typical work day, when his vessel was in port at Pearl Harbor, began aboard at roughly 6 A.M. and often didn't finish until nine or ten at night.

At sea, which was approximately half the time, his "work day" consumed twelve of every eighteen hours—six hours of sleep, a dozen of work, and so on week after week, in a continuous cycle of eighteen-hour "days" until the *San Francisco* was back in port and a customary twenty-four-hour schedule was resumed. To say that the work required a high degree of skill and training, as well as much endurance, would understate the situation. Moreover, the pay that my son received for his labors, fringe benefits plus salary, was niggardly by standards of the private sector. Many of his former college classmates were engaged by then in less demanding jobs on Wall Street and elsewhere, yet their pay routinely was double and triple his. This is not to say, of course, that he was unfairly treated. The choice of a military career was his alone to make, just as his various classmates presumably opted freely after college for their better paying civilian jobs. The point is, however, that many military people—the vast majority, I would guess—work exceedingly hard for very long hours. By and large, I would imagine, their productivity compares quite favorably with that of the most industrious employees to be found within the private sector.

To regard cutbacks in defense spending as a primary means of bringing the budget into closer balance is, in my opinion, shortsighted. Paring military outlays just isn't a valid way to begin to live within our means, at least not when the world continues to be so dangerous. Such budget-cutting seems once again the easy-way approach that has marked so much of our postwar behavior. The world remains dangerous even after summit meetings, and whatever prosperity we may manage to sustain in coming years will mean little if we lack the ability to defend ourselves and our allies.

In my view, it's a sorry reflection on the national mood that a 1984 public-opinion poll found 48 percent of Americans in favor of reducing military spending as the best means of cutting spending, while only 34 percent maintained that social-welfare expenditures should be trimmed.

It's no wonder that near Christmas 1985, Congress rushed through legislation—known as the Gramm-Rudman-Hollings deficit reduction plan—mandating budget cuts each

year through this decade in the event that rational reductions can't be agreed on. The plan, whose constitutionality
was promptly challenged in the courts, signified a clear abdi-
cation of political leadership, an absence of courage in the
Senate, the House, and the White House to withhold federal
largess in a sensible way, especially those handouts directed
to the comfortable and well-to-do.

INTEREST on the debt and the cost of defense account for
nearly 40 percent of all federal expenditures. But if these two
categories can't or shouldn't be cut, what can reasonably be
cut? Most of what's left falls into the human-resources group-
ing, which accounts for nearly half of all federal outlays. In
the 1980–85 period, spending in this category rose substantially, despite much talk about austerity and the hardships
that Reagan's budget-cutting supposedly was causing. But in
1980–85 spending for such programs as Social Security, Medicare, and federal retirement rose 17.3 percent, after inflation
adjustment. Much of this money, as we have seen, winds up
in middle-class and even wealthy households and is paid according to formulas laid down by law. No means test is involved. But even human-resource spending that requires a
means test increased in 1980–85 by 7.4 percent, after inflation. Like most federal expenditures, these programs to assist
the neediest have kept right on rising.
    Among the sharpest spending increases in 1980–85 were
farm price supports and rural-development subsidies, up 122
percent after inflation. Yet no sector of the population has
received more sympathetic treatment in print or broadcasting or on film in recent years than the occasionally depressed
farmers. A casual observer would suppose that Uncle Sam
had been miserly to agriculture—instead of remarkably generous—during the first four Reagan years. In 1984, less than
20 percent of all direct governmental aid to agriculture went
to farmers who were financially distressed. In other words,

for every $1 going to needy farmers, some $4 was winding up
with prosperous ones.

Also spurring the spending rise, it should be noted, is the
increasing role of mandatory cost-of-living adjustments
(COLA) in various federal programs. Currently, about 45
percent of the budget is indexed against inflation through
these so-called COLA arrangements. That's up from 26 percent in 1974. By linking Social Security and other such programs to the inflation rate, Congress is committed to
substantial benefit increases every year as far ahead as one
can see.

Some federal spending, at least in inflation-adjusted terms,
did decline in 1980–85. But this hardly suggests the emer-
gence of a national will to begin pulling in the belt. An example is spending on the infrastructure—highways, bridges,
water projects, mass-transit systems, and the like. Another is
spending to develop energy resources. In the long run, such
cutbacks could well limit, rather than spur, the economy's
overall growth. Like military cutbacks, these reductions may
seem relatively painless in the short run, but in the longer
term they can lead to serious difficulties.

OUR national reluctance to endure the pain of true austerity
can further be seen in budget-cutting attempts that ultimately failed. Consider, for example, the matter of Coast
Guard user fees. It's estimated that at least $1 billion could be
trimmed from the budget deficit if the Coast Guard were
required to charge the full freight for the various services
that it renders at sea, assisting everyone from the captain of
a huge commercial vessel to multimillionaire owners of plush
yachts to people such as me, who putter about in outboards
to fish.

Early in Reagan's first term, his administration proposed
that the Coast Guard begin charging fees for various services;
the proposal would have brought in perhaps $400 million, or

less than half the estimated value of the services that the Coast Guard renders gratis each year. Even among Republican legislators, however, the proposal received little support and was eventually scrapped in favor of successively scaled-down measures—first to collect $200 million in user fees and, when that failed, to take in only $60 million. After these bare-bones versions also failed to garner legislative support, the White House finally settled for as little as $8 million.

A similar fate befell a proposal aimed at curbing outlays by the federally funded Extension Service for agriculture, which operates in every county in the U.S., providing various sorts of instruction and other aid. However, many of its offices no longer are in farming regions, as originally arranged, but in suburbs and even urban centers. As a result, the agency's focus now is often on such matters as lawn care, gardening, and even home economics for apartment dwellers. The administration plan was to eliminate such nonfarm services of the agency by closing Extension offices where no farming was conducted. But the plan was soon abandoned for the usual political reasons.

The ranking Republican on the House appropriations subcommittee for agriculture happened to be Representative Virginia Smith of Nebraska, and she was dead against any such cutback. Aware of her legislative clout, the White House opted to scrap the plan. "Anything we took out, she'd put back in," a Reagan official told *Barron's* in early 1985. The magazine observed that "when it comes to agricultural subsidies and other farm programs, farm country Republicans can be as budget-busting as any farm country Democrat." In the case of the administration's Extension Service plan, of course, farmers themselves wouldn't have been affected; the impact would have fallen on suburbanites and city people. Nonetheless, that the agency was essentially farmer-oriented was enough to upset powerful farm-belt legislators on both sides of the congressional aisle.

The same irresolution marks most efforts to rein in other

federal expenditures. Anguish and eventual abandonment of belt-tightening attempts have been the usual outcome, however sensible proposed curtailments may have appeared. Take, for instance, the uproar that greeted White House plans to tighten up on federal loans to college students. To cut the budget deficit, the administration proposed ending government-subsidized loans for students in families earning more the $32,500 annually, as well as limiting any aid to no more than $4,000 per student. All in all, that hardly sounds like a plan devised by Ebeneezer Scrooge. Yet the anguish that it produced in the academic community, as well as elsewhere, was extraordinary.

No sooner was the proposal on the table than the president of Yale University, among other prominent college heads, was on the road to Washington to lambast the plan in Congress. Around the same time, in a most remarkable joint protest, the student-produced newspapers of the eight Ivy League colleges copublished an editorial blasting the White House idea. Elsewhere, the president of New York University, himself a former congressman, called the Reagan proposal "a declaration of war on American colleges and universities."

Meanwhile, the administration's new secretary of education, William J. Bennett, was excoriated in the press and on television for having the temerity to say in public what was plainly evident but rarely mentioned—that a very large portion of the nation's collegians were enjoying a very comfortable time of it on campuses from California to New York. The loan proposal, Bennett acknowledged, might indeed compel some families to "tighten the belt," but it might also "require from some students divestiture of certain sorts: stereo divestiture, automobile divestiture, three-weeks-at-the-beach divestiture." And he made the additional unmentionable point that, just possibly, too many people are going to college in the U.S. "Some people probably should not go," he declared, observing that "52 percent of our high school graduates go on to college, which is much higher than other countries; in Canada it's around 35 percent, and in Great Britain, Japan, and West Germany, it's around 15 percent." Bennett added: "If my own son, who is now ten months, came to me and said, 'You promised to pay tuition at Harvard; how about giving me $50,000 instead to start a little business?' I might think that was a good idea."

"Disastrous, Preposterous, Unconscionable" was the response in a magazine published at Trinity College, in Hartford. "If keeping a Trinity education in reach of those who aspire to one is important, let your senators and representatives know how you feel." The result of such outcries was a prompt move in the Senate to reject the White House plan. Lamenting such activity, in an editorial aptly titled "Groans of Academe," *The Wall Street Journal* noted that "the student-aid imbroglio has become so overblown that the most important point of the debate is obscured: The federal government will continue to offer educational assistance to the truly needy." Perhaps the sorriest episode in the entire student-loan saga occurred at the University of the Pacific, where the institution's president, Stanley McCaffrey, withdrew an invitation for Secretary Bennett to receive an honorary degree. "We simply cannot honor a person holding these views," McCaffrey explained.

Still another illustration of this national reluctance to curb spending can be glimpsed in an incident involving David Stockman, President Reagan's former budget director. Stockman blurted out in Congress at one point that all too many farmers seemed mainly concerned with federal bailouts rather than with agricultural endeavors. This remark, however accurate or inaccurate it may have been, produced instant outrage around the nation. Such reaction, in the spirit of the time, wasn't unusual. But it was extraordinary that Stockman's own mother, Carol, joined in the chorus of criticism. She rebuked her wayward son publicly, scolding him for suggesting that farmers were preoccupied with bail-outs.

Over an Iowa radio station, she reminded son David that his own parents were not only farmers but hard-pressed ones. She reminded him that his upbringing was on a family farm, and concluded with the admonition that his comments regarding farmers "do not set well with me." Stockman has since left the government to make his own millions as a writer and investment banker on Wall Street.[2]

SO far I have described efforts to trim expenditures, however feeble and unsuccessful. There are also countless instances where not even feeble stabs have been made. Untouched, for example, is a particularly outlandish Department of Agriculture project to develop tobacco for a "safe" cigarette, on which we have been spending more than $5 million annually, with no discernible results, though the effort persists at departmental laboratories in Beltsville, Maryland, Oxford, North Carolina, Athens, Georgia, and the University of Kentucky in Lexington. The federally funded effort has received no support from the tobacco industry, even though successful research could greatly benefit the industry. The reason, according to industry spokespeople, is that there's no proof that there's anything unsafe about the tobacco contained in present cigarettes.

Perhaps the most comprehensive survey of federal extravagance is the so-called Grace Commission report, formally titled the President's Private Sector Survey on Cost Control. Headed by J. Peter Grace—the head of the chemical firm bearing his name and cited earlier as among the corporations paying no tax—the commission labored long and hard to come up with ways in which federal funds could be conserved. The commission's six hundred fifty-page final report concluded that savings totaling nearly $425 billion in a three-year stretch were possible; about one third of this saving would be in general areas ranging from welfare to public works, one third in defense, and the balance in areas ranging from excessive travel costs at some federal agencies to over-use of the long-distance telephone at others.

In all, the commission raised 784 issues and put forward 2,478 specific recommendations. (Example: The Department of Energy, which Reagan officials once briefly talked of scrapping entirely, has one supervisor for every three employees, compared with a government-wide rate of one for seven; the department could save $19 million over three years by simply getting into line with the government-wide supervisor-employee ratio.)

As comprehensive as the Grace report is, its impact in curbing federal extravagance has been minimal. A headline in *The Wall Street Journal* near the end of Reagan's first term correctly relates the sorry story: "Grace on Federal 'Waste': Touted Report Won't Be Heeded." The article quotes legislators from both major parties who invariably praised the commission's work, but just as invariably went on to express doubt that many of the proposals could be adopted. Representative Pat Williams, a Montana Democrat, asserted that "the recommendations extract too much pain from middle-class America, and Congress will have no part of it." Representative Gene Taylor, a conservative Republican from Missouri, averred that "we all have to tighten our belts," but when pressed about specifics, he was quick to condemn a Grace proposal that would close twelve thousand rural post offices that serve fewer than one hundred people each. The report called for "less costly" alternatives, but Taylor, representing a rural Ozarks district, sarcastically inquired, "What alternatives? Carrier pigeons?"[3]

THERE are, of course, vast areas of federal spending that even the most enthusiastic budget-cutters concede should be cut little, if at all. One such area is huge indeed—the federal spending that goes to maintain and improve health care. The two main programs in this area—Medicare and Medicaid—

were launched as a part of the Great Society, and their perennial growth continues, whatever the particular status of
the federal budget. Spending for the two programs has risen
every year since their inception in the mid-1960s, and the
climb has actually accelerated in the last decade. At an annual rate of about $100 billion in 1985, the Medicare-Medicaid
total has expanded more than tenfold since the early 1970s,
and there's every reason to suppose that the growth will
continue despite some recent moves to have some recipients
shoulder slightly more of their expenses.

However wasteful and extravagant many federal programs may be, the government's health-care effort shows
admirable results. In July 1966, when Medicare took effect,
approximately half the nation's elderly population—sixty-
five years old and up—had no health insurance at all. Today,
virtually all are covered. Before Medicaid, the poor for whom
the program is maintained were seen by doctors an average
of 3.9 times a year, compared with a rate of 4.9 times for
other Americans. Now, according to a Johns Hopkins University study, "Medicaid recipients use physicians' services at
about the same level as most Americans."

In 1985, President Reagan proposed a temporary freeze on
Medicare payment rates for hospitals, a cut in certain special
allowances for teaching hospitals and an increase in Medicare premiums and deductibles for individuals using physicians' services. He also proposed a permanent limit on
federal payments to states for Medicaid. The proposal was
promptly rejected in the Republican-dominated Senate before even reaching the House, a considerably more liberal
body, where the opposition Democrats held a majority.

And so health-care outlays continue to mount. Estimates
show, for example, that Medicare's Hospital Insurance Trust
Fund, if nothing changes, will run short of funds to pay promised benefits by the end of this decade. By the mid-1990s,
the hospital insurance program is expected to be running at
a yearly deficit ranging from $200 billion to $400 billion. Yet

the problem was rarely raised on either side during the 1984 presidential campaign. Former Vice President Mondale promised, when the subject occasionally did surface, not to increase any Medicare-related charges and to maintain all benefits at least at current levels. The Reagan-Bush campaign assiduously eschewed the subject.

Such political tactics reflect a broad public attitude depicted in a 1985 survey by the nonprofit Conference Board. It found that most Americans opposed "any cuts in government spending for Social Security, health and medical care, and unemployment and child-care benefits." More than 80 percent of the three thousand households polled were against any reductions in the Social Security program, and as many as 75 percent opposed any health or medical-care cuts.

REAGAN'S rhetoric about the need to rein in spending is belied by his reluctance in his first term to use the veto, as the table shows:

PERIOD	PRESIDENT	VETOES PER YEAR	% SUSTAINED
1933–45	Roosevelt	52	99
1945–53	Truman	32	95
1953–61	Eisenhower	23	99
1961–63	Kennedy	7	100
1963–69	Johnson	6	100
1969–74	Nixon	8	86
1974–77	Ford	29	83
1977–81	Carter	8	94
1981–84	Reagan	7	83

As David R. Burton, a fiscal analyst at the U.S. Chamber of Commerce in Washington, has concluded: "Certainly, a profligate Congress deserves much of the blame for this sorry record [of federal extravagance], but Mr. Reagan himself deserves much of the blame—he has signed virtually every spending bill that Congress has presented to him."

To be entirely fair, the administration long requested—and was long denied—authority from Congress to employ the so-called line-item veto, which would allow Reagan to veto specific items in appropriations bills, choosing between specifics of a legislative spending proposal, striking out an obvious boondoggle here while letting pass a bona fide project there. In his 1985 budget speech, Reagan declared: "If Congress can't bring itself to do what's right, they should at least give me what forty-three governors already have—a line-item veto. Then I'll make cuts; I'll take the responsibility, and the heat, and I'll enjoy it."

The sentiment is noble, but it would have a more sincere ring if the presidential first-term record demonstrated a greater willingness to block spending. As the table shows, only one president—Lyndon Johnson—was more reluctant than Reagan to veto spending over the half century covered, and Johnson, unlike Reagan, made no bones about his eagerness to spend federal money.

Reagan's behavior reflects a broader national attitude; the president is a politician who aims to please, and his unwillingness to cut spending simply mirrors what his fellow Americans want. A *New York Times* / CBS News Poll taken in the spring of 1985 shows that opposition to spending cuts was greater among respondents earning over $50,000 a year than among those earning less. The survey found extensive support for a wide assortment of federal subsidies, such as to farmers, along with considerable support for reducing the budget deficit, but through reduced spending rather than higher taxes. However, when pressed for specifics on exactly where outlays might best be cut, most respondents wavered. Few managed to come up with suggestions that wouldn't prove personally harmful, and fewer still said they would support any such moves.

Another poll around the same time by *The Los Angeles*

Times turned up widespread reluctance to cut spending or raise taxes, with 87 percent of those queried opposed to any tinkering with cost-of-living adjustments in the Social Security program and 81 percent opposed to closing down the Small Business Administration, a federal agency widely viewed by experts as superfluous. Large majorities also opposed any cuts in such other programs as general revenue sharing, the Veterans Administration, health care, or federal civil service salaries. At the same time, the Roper organization found that 77 percent of Americans opposed Reagan proposals, later abandoned, to tax health insurance and other employee benefits; some 60 percent of those queried added that they would be unlikely to vote for any congressional candidate who favored the Reagan plan.

With the electorate in such a mood, and in the absence of sound leadership in Washington, it's not surprising that the nation should find itself in early 1986 with a ludicrous piece of legislation—Gramm-Rudman-Hollings—designed to cut spending and balance the budget in such a manner that no single politician or political party could be directly blamed for any resulting discomfort. Apart from questions about its constitutionality—for instance, its failure to distinguish between the executive and legislative branches with such provisions as spending cuts to be made by the General Accounting Office—the measure cast doubt on our capacity to pull in the belt in a rational way. It was akin to a diet in which food is rationed without regard to what sort—a pound of ice cream weighs the same as a pound of grapefruit.

Such programs cannot succeed, of course, and we are left once again with the need to restrain ourselves through sensible, if painful, ways. But there's little to suggest that the fortitude for such a process exists in Washington or elsewhere. And without that, our extravagance is bound ultimately to overwhelm us.

Chapter 7

Debt Rolls On

To bring borrowing under any sort of real control appears even less likely than to control spending, which, as we've seen, is itself unlikely. To borrow is as American as apple pie. The biggest and best of America's institutions enthusiastically encourage the practice. Michael Thomas, writing about business for *Manhattan Inc.*, reported in a 1985 column that in twelve months he received invitations—all unsolicited— to own as many as twenty credit cards. My own experience is similar, and the senders read like a *Who's Who* of U.S. business, ranging from Mobil Corp. to Sears, Roebuck & Co.

The largest bank-card issuer is Citicorp, with some eleven million charge-card accounts. First Chicago Corp. has some three million cards outstanding, a 30 percent rise in two years. Often, such institutions find card customers simply by mailing out preapproved cards, based on magazine subscription lists and the like. The Bank of New Orleans once even sent credit cards to a group of potential credit customers who, according to the bank's computers, had steady jobs. And so they did, as inmates working at Angola State Prison, 125 miles northwest of New Orleans. Citicorp once mailed an unsolicited card to an eighteen-year-old girl who had just graduated from high school and had no job or savings.

This pushing of credit cards willy-nilly on so many consumers has contributed greatly to the rise of consumer debt—as well as of consumer debt losses. Such losses at larger banks —those with assets of at least $300 million—reached $2.5 billion in the first half of 1985, nearly twice the level of the year earlier. Home Federal Savings & Loan of San Diego—after mailing cards with credit lines of up to $5,000 to people with no jobs or poor credit ratings—faced some $30 million in consumer losses in late 1985. It blamed about half the losses on people who couldn't service their credit-card borrowing. Similarly, Citicorp wrote off $492 million of consumer debt in the first nine months of 1985, more than double the amount of the year earlier. At BankAmerica Corp., the ratio of consumer-loan losses to losses on commercial loans, at one to five in 1984, had moved in late 1985 to about one in two, and the bank pinned much of the blame on credit-card problems.[1]

In all, nearly $50 billion of some $2.6 trillion of consumer debt was past due in 1985. The Federal Reserve has authority under the Credit Control Act of 1969 to place restraints on borrowing, and in the spring of 1980, as interest rates soared, the Fed acted, with President Carter's blessing, to limit borrowing, implementing measures to restrain the growth of certain types of consumer and business credit, including credit-card activity. Among other things, it required all types of lenders—including those soliciting would-be credit-card holders—to maintain on deposit at a Federal Reserve bank a minimum percentage of any increases in credit-card lending or other sort of unsecured consumer credit. It also raised the so-called marginal reserve requirement on short-term time deposits of $100,000 or more at large commercial banks.

Credit growth did abate in the ensuing weeks, and by early July President Carter revoked the Fed's authority under the Credit Control Act. By that time, however, overall business activity was in a deepening recession that many analysts attributed in large part to the credit-control measures. As Carter ended the controls, the economy seemed to be in a nose dive, and a presidential election would take place in November. With the curbs lifted and credit once more increasing, the economy soon revived, and a new business upturn was under way by late summer of 1980. The volume of consumer installment credit outstanding, which had fallen some $6 billion before the credit controls were lifted, rose by nearly $4 billion in the year's final months.

The Carter administration had come eyeball to eyeball with the nation's addiction to credit and blinked. Addiction may seem too strong a word for a way of doing business that has greatly facilitated our remarkable postwar expansion. Without liberal credit, prosperity would have come a good deal harder. But the brush with controls in early 1980 shows that withdrawal from the long postwar borrowing binge is simply too painful in an economy as accustomed to affluence as ours. So we lifted the controls and let the debt continue to pile up. Prolonged abuse of a narcotic usually will end in disaster, and so will overuse of credit. As Wilkins Micawber put it in *David Copperfield,* "Annual income twenty pounds, annual expenditure nineteen and six, result happiness; annual income twenty pounds, annual expenditure twenty ought and six, result misery."

We have depended far too long on overborrowing to sustain our postwar prosperity. It's impossible to say precisely when the point of no return was passed, but it assuredly predates early 1980, when Carter invoked credit controls. And it no longer appears possible to avoid a denouement along the approximate lines that Mr. Micawber suggests, for debt so permeates our economy now that it can no longer be liquidated in an orderly fashion.

DEBT, as we have seen, has grown with little interruption since the war. The new, increasingly disturbing element, however, is that deepening financial difficulties accompany this growth. In mid-1985, past-due debt referred to one New York collection agency, a unit of Dun & Bradstreet, was running 37 percent above the previous year, even though the level of business activity had risen in the interim. Another collection agency, the Chilton Corp. of Dallas, reported that its funds-recovery rate had dropped to 27 percent, from 31 percent a year before. A Chilton executive called the pattern "spooky, to say the least." Ivan Christy, the owner of a Denver agency, found a similar trend in his area. "A lot of people that we see now are second- or third-generation bad-debtors," he told *The Wall Street Journal,* and added that "people just aren't used to living on what they make anymore."

A poll taken in 1984 by the New York securities firm of Becker Paribas Inc. found that only 64.3 percent of a cross section of leading financial officers regarded the U.S. banking system as "fundamentally sound." This was down from 76.5 percent in December 1983. And only 45.6 percent of the 378 officials viewed the international banking system as sound. "Imprudent lending" was cited as the main reason. This is more in keeping with the Great Depression than a supposedly prosperous time.

In June 1985, the assets of more than four hundred savings-and-loan associations barely exceeded their liabilities, according to a government survey. Of 3,150 federally insured savings and loans, perhaps one third would disappear by 1990, the report estimated. However, depositors would presumably emerge unscathed because the Federal Savings and Loan Insurance Corp. (FSLIC) stood behind the associations. The FSLIC, like the Federal Deposit Insurance Corp., is a government agency that insures deposits up to $100,000 each. As recently as 1981, the survey indicated, fewer than eighty savings and loans were in such dire straits that their assets barely covered their liabilities.

In early May 1985, people in Maryland who happened to have money on deposit in any of that state's 102 privately insured savings-and-loan associations learned firsthand what can happen when a thrift institution becomes overextended. Their deposits had no FSLIC backing if trouble developed— as it did. On May 15, Maryland Governor Harry R. Hughes imposed a $1,000-a-month limit on depositor withdrawals from the institutions, as part of an effort to stem an old-fashioned depression-style run. The governor's drastic action came on the heels of reports of management problems at one of the larger savings institutions, and after the Maryland associations as a whole had lost some $630 million of deposits within several months. The drain on May 13 alone came to $116 million.

In the days just before the limit was mandated, long lines of depositors, some waiting overnight, had been forming at the beleaguered units around the state. One couple, Joe and Mary Piechota, waited in line for nine hours to get their money out of Old Court Savings & Loan of Baltimore. Parking lots outside suburban Baltimore-area savings and loans were littered with the lawn chairs and picnic coolers of savers seeking to rescue their money. George Becker, the thirty-five-year-old business manager of a car dealership in Baltimore, was one of a hundred individuals waiting outside Fairfax Savings & Loan Association in Pikesville, Md. "The bottom line is it's a panic scare," he remarked while waiting.

The repercussions rippled far beyond families unfortunate enough to have money in the associations. Public utilities serving the area—Chesapeake & Potomac Telephone Cos., Washington Gas Light Co., and Potomac Electric Power Co. —were compelled to announce that if customers couldn't pay their bills because of restrictions imposed on their bank accounts, they should call customer service offices to arrange for delayed billing. At the same time, such major retailers in the area as Giant Food and Safeway Stores cut back on their check-cashing facilities for customers wishing to cash checks that were written on the troubled associations.

The Maryland crisis didn't have a Great Depression ending. Through stopgap measures and with federal help, the depositors didn't actually lose money. Nor does it rival the sort of financial crises that struck occasionally in the nineteenth and early twentieth centuries, before the creation of the Federal Reserve System. Consider, for instance, the situation described in the Jan. 18, 1842, issue of the *Public Ledger*.

The article depicts the anger of depositors at the Bank of Cincinnati, whose notes they wished to exchange "for the paper of some other and less suspicious institutions." The report states that the "crowd gradually increased to several hundred by 9 o'clock," the opening hour, at which time a notice was "stuck on the door of the banking house." It carried the news that the bank "had suspended payment for 20 days." In the ensuing hours, the incensed depositors stormed the bank, and "commenced demolition of everything they could lay their hands on—books, papers, desks and counters. . . ." Later, according to the report, the local sheriff appeared, only to be driven off while the bank's main vault was "attacked with crowbars, sledgehammers, etc."

Such was not the scene in Maryland. Still, the resemblances between Maryland in May 1985 and the U.S. as a whole in the 1930s, as well as in earlier times, is disquieting. Nor was the Maryland situation unique. It came in the wake of a similar crisis in Ohio, where depositors of Home State Savings Bank had to be reimbursed some $175 million. About two thirds of this was provided by the state government, and the rest through aid from other thrift institutions. Home Savings had loaned securities to a government bond dealer that failed, and when the word got out, frightened depositors started lining up early in the morning, as in Maryland. Several other, smaller Ohio-based institutions experienced similar runs. As in Maryland, the Ohio deposits weren't federally insured. In both states, fortunately, such privately insured deposits were relatively small when the trouble hit. They totaled about $9 billion in Maryland and close to $5 billion in Ohio. Still, roughly five hundred thousand Ohio savers were trapped briefly without access to all their funds, and an even larger number of Maryland residents were in similar straits.

THE crises in Maryland and Ohio were not the only evidence of strain in the financial system in the mid-1980s. Data supplied by the Federal Savings and Loan Insurance Corp. show that the savings-and-loan industry as a whole sustained losses on real estate loans of nearly $1.5 billion in the first half of 1985, more than twice the loss level of the year before. At the time, 200 savings associations accounted for more than half the losses, and 145 of these were regarded as having no real capital; their liabilities exceeded their assets. But to close these units would have required as much as three times the FSLIC's unobligated bailout reserve of $3.2 billion. Instead of taking such action, the agency managed to place many of the beleaguered associations under the wings of healthier thrift institutions. The upshot was to weaken the financial structure of the sounder units, while limiting the drain on FSLIC reserves. At best, the maneuver was a stopgap procedure that did nothing to correct the underlying problem of excessive and unwise real estate borrowing.

In residential real estate, home mortgage delinquency data also reflect mounting financial strain. The Mortgage Bankers Association in Washington reported in mid-1985 that 6.19 percent of all home mortgages had fallen thirty days or more into arrears during the preceding quarter. This was the highest figure in the more than two decades that the association, which represents banks and savings institutions, has monitored such data. The association also reported that in the same quarter, lenders had begun foreclosure proceedings on .24 percent of all home loans, still a relatively small figure, but high by postwar standards. The pattern makes clear that the real-estate market is still another economic area where debt difficulties have intensified dangerously.

A year before the crises in Maryland and Ohio, in 1984, one of the nation's largest and most respected commercial banks —Continental Illinois National Bank & Trust Co. of Chicago —came within a whisker of having to close down. On May 10, rumors spread that Continental Illinois was in serious financial trouble. On the next day, the bank was forced to borrow some $3.6 billion from the Federal Reserve Bank of Chicago in order to stay solvent. In the following couple of days, emergency calls were made to other commercial banks across the country in an effort to round up more cash. A group of sixteen banks agreed to offer Continental $4.5 billion in credit available over a thirty-day period; at the same time, the Fed pumped many more billions into the staggering bank. Finally, on May 17, the government rescued Continental. The Federal Deposit Insurance Corp. injected $1.5 billion, and another $500 million was provided by other banks. In addition, the Fed and the FDIC guaranteed that no Continental depositor—even those with more than $100,000 in their accounts—would lose a penny on deposit at the bank. At the same time, an additional $1 billion of credit was provided by the bank group, whose participants meanwhile had swelled to twenty-eight banks.

This was the largest such rescue effort ever put together in U.S. banking. And it was hardly conducted out of altruism. The participating banks were keenly aware that if Continental Illinois failed, one of them could well be the next to go under. At the time, Continental was one of the ten largest commercial banks in the country. The root of the 137-year-old institution's problem was that in striving to adopt a less stodgy, more aggressive image, it had purchased more than $1 billion of energy-related loans from a relatively small Oklahoma City institution called Penn Square Bank. When Penn Square was unable to meet its obligations, as the energy business soured during the 1981–82 recession, Continental was compelled to write off much of $1 billion. And there were other bad loans. By the start of 1984's second quarter, Continental's problem loans amounted to $2.3 billion, or nearly 8 percent of all its loans outstanding. The average for other major commercial banks at the time was about 2.5 percent.

A footnote to the Continental story is that the bank had been rescued by the government once before, in 1932, with a $50 million infusion of preferred stock from the federal government's Reconstruction Finance Corp. Walter Cummings, the bank's chairman in much of the difficult depression era, was careful to shun unsound loans and invested the bulk of the bank's money as conservatively as possible, much of it in government bonds. In 1939, he was able to retire the preferred stock and thus win back independence for the bank, an independence that once again ended in the spring of 1984.[2]

Signs of financial strain at commercial banks by no means disappeared after the Continental crisis. On a single day—Friday, May 31, 1985—no fewer than seven banks failed in four states: Nebraska, Oregon, Arkansas, and Minnesota. This was the most to fail in a day since the Great Depression. The FDIC had little difficulty, to be sure, in finding buyers; over that weekend, five of the seven were taken over by other institutions. However, the other two banks, both in Nebraska, were scheduled for liquidation, with the FDIC arranging to make good on outstanding deposits up to $100,000 per account. Alan Whitney, an FDIC official, stated at the time that "the principal factor in the closings stems from poor management practices, including liberal lending policies, failure to assess the ability of borrowers to repay loans and [failure] to take account of the declining value of farmland as collateral." These seven failures brought the total number of failures in 1985, with only five months gone, to forty-three banks. This was on top of seventy-nine failures in all of 1984 and forty-eight in all of 1983. For all of 1985, there were 120 bank failures, and the 1986 total reached about 150.

THE decline in farmland values, alluded to by Whitney of the FDIC, has been traced by the Federal Reserve Bank of Chicago. In the first quarter of 1985, according to the Chicago Fed, these values in the key Seventh Federal Reserve District, centered in Illinois, were fully 18 percent lower than a year before and as much as one third below the 1981 peak. "Bankers believe that further declines are in store," stated the Chicago Reserve Bank's monthly "Agricultural Letter." The only parallel to such a drop, the letter continued, "is the 13-year slide in farmland values that began in 1920, following the boom conditions that prevailed through World War I. During that particularly distressful period in the history of U.S. agriculture, farmland prices nationwide fell more than 55 percent. After bottoming in the depths of the Great Depression, farmland values edged up [and] in the early 1950s finally topped the 1920 high."

In 1985, commercial banks held one third of all outstanding farm debt, which approximated $180 billion. The remainder was accounted for largely by the Cooperative Farm Credit System, comprising Federal Land Banks, Production Credit Associations, and Banks for Cooperatives. In early 1985, according to the office of the comptroller of the currency, 26 percent of these commercial banks lending to farmers were classified as "needing special attention" on account of bad loans. "The condition of agricultural banks will continue to deteriorate," the report stated, adding that "the number of problem agricultural bank failures will continue to grow." Too many farmers had borrowed too heavily and couldn't make interest payments, let alone repay principal.

By any yardstick, farm debt has worsened severely in the 1980s. In 1981, there were some forty problem banks in farm areas. Four years later, the total was close to four hundred. Of all problem banks in 1981, about 20 percent were farm banks, so called because at least a quarter of their loans are to farmers. Four years later, the percentage had doubled. In mid-1985, as much as half the approximately $51 billion that farmers owed to bankers was viewed as "dangerously delinquent," according to one study. Some 13.5 percent of Bank of America's $1.7 billion in farm loans was at least ninety days past due in the spring of 1985; the comparable past-due rate at the end of 1984 was 10.5 percent.

Through farm failures and foreclosures, banks have been accumulating farmland at a swifter clip than since the Great Depression. In Iowa, for instance, banks held some $153 million of farm real estate in early 1985, one third more than a year earlier. But for regulatory leniency, the number would be far higher. Moreover, Iowa state legislators in 1984 passed a law permitting banks to hold on to real estate for five years; previously, the rules required that such holdings be sold within one year. Thomas Huston, Iowa's banking superintendent, has forecast further farmland price declines, and that banks will continue to be saddled with additional hard-to-sell farmland. "We're in for a hell of a whipping," Huston predicts.

Huston first began cautioning Iowans as early as 1980 that the value of their farmland might decline. At the same time, he warned local bankers that loans based on speculative land valuations might lead to credit problems down the road. His advice was largely disregarded, despite the fact that Huston himself farms 340 acres in Iowa's Washington County. Land values there fell 30 percent, to $1,574 an acre, in a recent four-year period. Huston also is president of a family-controlled bank with assets of some $40 million, located at Columbus Junction, a small town whose economy still feels the shock of the 1983 closing of a local meatpacking plant that provided 250 jobs.[3]

THE continuing rise of farm debt is similar to the rise in debt that American banks now face in many less-developed third world countries. As in the case of farm loans, all too often these loans to third world countries have been unwisely negotiated, pressed on the less-developed areas in some instances by bankers interested only in the high rates to be earned and not the attendant perils. Latin America alone carries an external debt of some $360 billion, by a recent estimate, much of it pressed on the various Latin countries

by U.S. commercial banks in the 1970s, in an effort to recycle
funds pouring in from the newly rich oil-exporting countries
in the Middle East. At more than $50 billion, the correspond-
ing debt total for the tropical African countries is smaller but
still huge. Third world debt prompted finance ministers of
the British Commonwealth nations, meeting in Toronto in
late 1984, to issue a warning that "the world's financial system
is balanced on a knife edge; the present situation is not sus-
tainable."

Two major factors have thus far prevented this buildup of
third world debt from turning into a massive credit collapse.
One is the determination of banks and such governmental
institutions as the Federal Reserve and the International
Monetary Fund to keep pumping new money into the
strapped countries and to reschedule outstanding loans. The
other is the remarkable willingness of third world borrowers
to adopt austerity measures, voluntarily or at the request of
such organizations as the IMF.

As an analysis in *The Bank Credit Analyst,* the Montreal-
based monthly economic report, wisely cautions, however,
"it would be rash to believe that these two factors can be
relied upon to keep the [third world] debt problem manageable indefinitely, much less provide any sort of long-run resolution." The analysis notes that austerity has already brought
sporadic flare-ups in some Latin American lands. Among the
bloodiest of these protests against austerity was a 1984 riot in
the Dominican Republic. At the time, the island country's
gross national product, on a per capita basis, was only $1,515,
about one tenth the levels prevailing in the world's most
prosperous nations.

The U.S. also has suffered in this situation. Wharton Economic Forecasting Associates Inc. estimates that in 1981–84
some eight hundred thousand American jobs were lost as a
direct result of the Latin American debt crisis. U.S. exports
to Latin America "deteriorated from $39 billion in 1981 to
$26.3 billion in 1984" as countries in the region restricted

their imports of U.S. goods in order to husband their dollars for debt repayment.

The bind that excessive borrowing causes for these less-developed lands is evident, among other places, in the extent to which their export earnings cover their debt-service costs. A dozen years ago, economists grew concerned when a less-developed country was forced to spend perhaps 20 percent of its yearly export income to service its medium- plus long-term bank borrowing. By 1984, however, forty of eighty-one countries surveyed by Morgan Guaranty Trust Co. showed borrowing rates of more than 20 percent on such debt. The rates for Zaire, Argentina, Mexico, Chile, Brazil, and Morocco approximated 50 percent. With short-term debt also included, the rates exceeded 100 percent of export earnings in some instances. The rate touched 200 percent in the case of Argentina and 150 percent-plus in the Philippines, Uruguay, Israel, and Mexico.

Two developments in the mid-1980s tended to ease the debt burden for some of these nations. The oil-price spiral, which helped bring on the bind in the 1970s, didn't resume. Oil prices tumbled, in fact, and this has served to reduce energy costs in many of the poorest borrowing countries, where petroleum consumption depends largely on imported supplies. In addition, interest rates dropped appreciably, along with an easing of inflation, and this tended to lighten the borrowing burden. A rough rule of thumb holds that every one half percentage point rise in the rate at which these countries can borrow funds costs them an extra $1 billion.

Against these welcome developments must be weighed less heartening considerations. Many of the most indebted countries are simply not managing to achieve a level of exporting necessary to service their debt for any sustained period. In mid-1985, the combined trade surplus of Argentina, Brazil, Mexico, and Venezuela—the largest debtors in the Latin American area—was lagging 24 percent behind levels of the year before. The largest declines were in Mexico, a major oil producer, whose surplus fell from $12.8 billion to $8.4 billion in the twelve months, and in Brazil, where it dropped from $13.1 billion to $10.5 billion. Factors in such declines ranged from sluggishness in economic growth in the all-important U.S. market to persistent weakness in prices of many raw materials—particularly oil—produced by such nations.

As the third world debt burden has grown, so have cries for repudiation of the debt. An early proponent of repudiation was Cuba's Fidel Castro, who has argued that the debt is unpayable, and in any case, ordinary citizens should not be bound to make good on loans whose proceeds were squandered by their rich countrymen. He softened his position somewhat in an interview with Arthur Schlesinger Jr., reported in *The Wall Street Journal* in mid-1985. Castro said, "The solution will be for the industrialized countries to take over the debts owed to private banks if bankruptcy of the financial system is to be prevented. . . . The banks would recover the capital they had invested, U.S. export companies would increase their exports, and U.S. investors would increase their profits."[4] In other words, Uncle Sam must solve the crisis by bailing out the commercial banks that have lent so much so unwisely over the years.

There are few precedents for outright repudiation of debt by a sovereign nation. When the Bolsheviks reneged after the 1917 Russian Revolution on debts run up by the czars, the U.S. froze Russian assets in the U.S. In the early part of Franklin D. Roosevelt's presidency, a settlement of sorts was negotiated between the U.S. and Russia, but the creditors weren't actually paid until 1959, and then at a repayment rate of only ten cents per dollar owed. In the event of a repudiation now, U.S. bankers would presumably seek to impound such items as shipments of grain from the debtor country arriving at U.S. ports, any of its aircraft at U.S. airports, and any of its bank branches within the U.S. Bankers also maintain that they would be able to halt most money transfers to or from the debtor nation so that it could neither make nor receive payments abroad. This would mean, for example, that if the debtor country happened to buy its oil from British Petroleum and tried to pay BP, an intervening bank would freeze the payment. Seizing a country's overseas holdings, of course, is a desperate move, as is repudiation of foreign debt, and there are many in-between measures for debtor nations, short of outright refusal to pay. Mexico has resorted to a moratorium, for example, and Argentina to frequent rescheduling of payments. Debtor nations may agree to repay more than their exports are taking in for a time, but in the longer run such a situation clearly cannot persist.

Whether or not repudiation is attempted on a wide scale, third world debt is another aspect of America's financial bind. "The U.S. banking system can survive [third world] loan defaults only if the Federal Reserve manages to isolate the international financial system from the domestic," according to a Data Resources analysis. "The position of the major money center banks could be precarious." The nine largest of these banks, which until 1984 included Continental Illinois, all recently had more than 100 percent of their outstanding equity in third world loans. In theory, third world defaults on a large scale would render many of these banks insolvent. In practice, the Fed would surely take drastic measures to shore up the institutions and prevent panic among depositors.

Data Resources provides estimates on the degree of big-bank loan exposure. Focusing on four countries—Argentina, Brazil, Mexico, and Venezuela—the analysis places their combined debt at 135 percent of equity at Citibank, 158 percent at Bank of America, 162 percent at Chase Manhattan Bank, 193 percent at Manufacturers Hanover, 139 percent at Morgan Guaranty, 141 percent at Chemical Bank, 162 percent at Bankers Trust, and 128 percent at First Chicago. The report also shows the average debt-to-equity reading for all commercial banks in the U.S., at 49 percent, to be far under the corresponding levels at most of the large money-center banks.

Looking ahead, the Mexican situation particularly suggests the degree of difficulty entailed in overlending to third world nations. In late 1985, Mexican finance officials told American bankers in New York that Mexico would need some $10 billion in new bank loans over the following three years, with $2.5 billion of that needed in 1986. The request falls within the purview of the so-called Baker plan. Named for Treasury secretary James Baker, this plan was launched in October 1985 by the Reagan administration in order to prevent third world defaults. It calls for banks in the U.S. as well as abroad to supply some $20 billion over three years to fifteen debtor nations, chiefly in Latin America. Thus, the Mexican borrowing alone would consume fully half of the total proposed by Baker to handle all third world debt troubles. But Mexico until 1985 had been viewed as a model for other third world countries seeking to work out of debt difficulties. As its loan request indicates, the Mexican government was simply unable to perform the belt-tightening necessary. Moreover, a few months before the New York meeting, the peso plunged from two hundred to the dollar to five hundred to the dollar.

LET'S turn now to corporate debt. Junk bonds are corporate-debt issues judged too risky for conservative investments by the main rating services, Moody's and Standard & Poor's. But by 1985, junk bonds had become a standard feature in the portfolios of many insurance firms, savings-and-loan associations, and pension funds. Between 1979 and 1984, the yearly amount of junk bonds issued rose from $2 billion to $15 billion. In early 1986, junk-bond debt outstanding approached $85 billion. The appeal of such securities is twofold. They carry significantly higher interest rates than their less risky counterparts. And they have played a key role in the corporate takeover game that has pervaded Wall Street. Their function has been to finance highly leveraged, hostile corporate acquisitions. This financing has often taken the form of unregistered, unrated, or lowly rated debt, issued by "shell" corporations created especially as vehicles for hostile takeover attempts.

In early 1985, such tactics were employed in an effort by Turner Broadcasting to take over CBS, a far larger, more prestigious company; the effort, which eventually failed, involved $5.4 billion in junk takeover bonds. Around the same time, there was an attempt by Mesa Partners II to gain control of Unocal Corp., involving $3 billion in junk bonds. Nicholas F. Brady, chairman of Dillon, Read & Co., a New York investment banker, conceded at the time that many of his Wall Street colleagues were lucratively engaged in the junk-bond game. Yet, he warned, "Junk takeover financing, which is largely devoted to unproductive purposes, dangerously threatens to destabilize America's national savings system." When major investors, he added, "reach for higher yields without regard for security and safety of principal, the results can be disastrous."

To gain control of another company, typically, a corporation will replace equity with debt, an exchange actually encouraged by U.S. tax regulations, which allow interest payments to be deducted from pre-tax income while dividends must be paid out of after-tax income. Thus, debt can be much cheaper than equity capital, and this provides a tempting arrangement for takeover plotters. How all this works can be seen, for instance, in the recent acquisition of National Can by Triangle Industries, in which Triangle replaced $460 million of National Can equity with only $70 million of its own and raised most of the rest of the takeover money through high-interest junk bonds. Triangle's new debt represented over 90 percent of its total capital and, at about 15 percent interest, servicing it should run about $55 million yearly through the balance of this decade. Pre-tax earnings of the two firms, which totaled $72 million in 1984, can be used for debt servicing, but in addition, Triangle will probably need from time to time to sell off assets to keep up with the debt payments. If business softens, of course, debt payments can't be trimmed or eliminated, except through default, while dividends can always be cut.

Ultimately, such debt-leveraged takeovers reduce a company's margin for error if the economy or the particular industry turns sour, for the result of these mergers is to substitute debt for permanent capital—precisely the opposite of sound, forward-looking financial policy. The number of such leveraged deals reached about 250 in 1985, up from 164 three years before, and the value of the largest of such takeovers rose in the period to about $20 billion from $3.5 billion. Alarmed by the pattern, the Federal Reserve Board moved in late 1985 to tighten the rules for such financing, but it remained doubtful whether such action would arrest the trend. In any event, by the time the Fed decided to move, the general credit structure of many major corporations had been extensively weakened.

In early 1986, four firms in the oil business, for example, were unable to service their junk-bond debt, and defaults on such securities climbed over $1 billion. Global Marine Inc. accounted for $340 million of the total. Other junk-bond issuers in default at the time made up a diverse group, including Elsinore Corp., a gaming company, Oak Industries Inc., a cable TV operator, Sharon Steel Corp., and Brock Hotel Corp. John Shad, the chairman of the Securities & Exchange Commission in 1985 as the junk-bond boom was mounting, remarks, "The more leveraged takeovers and buyouts today, the more bankruptcies tomorrow."[5]

MEANWHILE, the U.S. itself has joined the ranks of debtor nations. This slide from creditor to debtor status was the result of vast inflows throughout the early 1980s of foreign money, seeking investment in America and attracted by the relatively high interest rates available. These inflows, in turn, reflected a return of American dollars spent abroad for goods and services.

This transformation to debtor status marked the first time since World War I that America has owed more to countries abroad than they owed it. When a nation, be it the U.S. or any other, moves from creditor to debtor status, the need to service its global debt obligations sooner or later places pressure on it to export more and import less, as many third world countries have discovered. As a result, the economy of a debtor nation grows increasingly vulnerable to withdrawals of foreign investment. In the case of the U.S., such investment in the early and mid-1980s enabled Uncle Sam to finance huge federal budget deficits relatively painlessly. Foreigners flocked to purchase U.S. corporate and Treasury issues that otherwise would have had to be sold to Americans, presumably at higher interest rates. Possibly, the Federal Reserve Board would have also had to buy more Treasury issues, which would have acted to drive up the money supply and ultimately fuel inflation. The dollar, in such circumstances, would tend to slump on foreign-exchange markets. Worse still, American companies seeking investment funds for expansion projects would find themselves competing more directly with the U.S. Treasury.

In 1984, net financial investment by foreigners in U.S. securities markets—stocks, bonds, and so on—totaled $68.5 billion, up from $26.7 billion in 1983 and a minus reading of $34.3 billion in 1982. These sums dwarf the $26.8 billion of federal debt acquired by foreigners in 1984. The Institute for International Economics, a Washington research group, reckons that the U.S. will owe in interest alone some $100 billion annually to foreigners by 1989. By then, assuming no big changes in general economic trends, the U.S. will have accumulated $1 trillion of debt owed to the rest of the world. In such an event, the U.S. would be increasingly vulnerable, for example, to credit strains in foreign financial markets. Meantime, foreign investors would presumably come to view U.S. securities as more and more risky, inasmuch as the U.S. economy would be increasingly at the mercy of financial conditions elsewhere. Should foreigners withdraw the bulk of their funds, the resulting shortage of investment money could cause a severe squeeze in U.S. credit markets and restrict new capital projects.

THE overriding impression, as one surveys the buildup of debt across the entire spectrum of U.S. economic activity, is that the dimensions are simply overwhelming. They exceed the capacity—as great as it may be—of even governmental agencies to cope. They also exceed the capacity of the U.S. economy to grow its way out of this problem, as some supply-side economists claim is possible. If the U.S. were to grow at some 5 percent annually year after year after year, then just possibly the prosperity generated by such sustained, brisk growth would be sufficient to render this debt bearable and, eventually, even manageable. But U.S. economic history makes clear that such perennial growth simply won't happen, particularly when there is such a need to pare budgetary red ink. Budget-cutting tends to retard rather than spur economic growth.

As the mountain of debt keeps rising, the credit of the U.S. isn't infinite. There's a limit to the ability of private and even governmental insurance agencies to bail everybody out all the time. In an interview with the editors of *U.S. News & World Report* in 1984, William Isaac, then chairman of the Federal Deposit Insurance Corp., asserted that, notwithstanding proliferating failures, "the banking system is completely safe." He stressed that the Federal Reserve is always available to provide liquidity to the banking system in the event that the FDIC, for instance, should be unable to meet depositors' claims, as happened in the case of Continental

Illinois. But the FDIC official neglected to explain what backing there is behind the Fed itself.

The Fed's capacity to bail out strapped organizations lies, of course, in its ability, as a central bank, to create money. But in the event of snowballing bankruptcies, would the Fed really be able to perform that task in a fashion that would permit the economy to keep operating smoothly? No one knows, but my guess is that the Fed wouldn't be able to perform the necessary rescue operations, at least not in a relatively painless manner, one that would permit the economy to keep running smoothly along.

Federal Reserve Chairman Paul A. Volcker reflected this worry in an address at the Harvard commencement ceremonies in June 1985. He expressed concern that too many Americans have come to take the financial system—and the government's capacity to bail out all debtors—for granted. He noted that such institutions as the FDIC, the FSLIC, and the Fed itself arose as a direct result of financial crises in the nineteenth and early twentieth centuries, to provide a kind of financial safety net. This, he asserted, is all to the good. However, he went on, there are limits even to the capacity of the various governmental institutions. He lamented the spreading attitude of banks and other private organizations that come what may, they will be protected by Uncle Sam from any catastrophic consequences that imprudent lending might otherwise cause. "There has to be a better way," he declared. But he didn't proffer any, other than to urge "a stronger sense of business integrity and fiduciary responsibility." That may be a worthy goal, but the pattern of postwar America suggests that it's most unlikely to be achieved.

In a similar vein, Henry Kaufman, the noted chief economist of Salomon Brothers Inc., told a congressional committee in mid-1985 that "we are drifting toward a financial system that has no guardian." The various deposit-insurance arrangements, which seemed laudable in the 1930s, have served lately, he said, "to remove the link" of responsibility between creditor and borrower. The upshot, he warned, is "a world of unrestrained credit growth." He also lamented the spread of "credit lines and guarantees in which the insurers' credit exposures are often only an off-balance-sheet item." In this regard, a 1985 study by the FDIC shows that the nation's fifteen largest banks, led by Citibank, Bank of America, and Chase Manhattan, have accumulated nearly $1 trillion in liabilities not to be found on their balance sheets. These include such obligations as bank-issued guarantees and commitments to make loans and purchase foreign exchange. Commenting on the report, Irvine H. Sprague, an FDIC director, remarks that "the raw numbers are a little scary." In other words, as shaky as the banks' published balance-sheet statements may be, the true situation is even shakier.

A few statistics help underline the inadequacy of the first line of defense in the event of snowballing credit difficulties. In 1984, the FDIC had reserves totaling only $15.4 billion, against insured deposits of about $1.3 trillion. And the similar organization for savings-and-loan associations, the Federal Savings & Loan Insurance Corp., had $63 billion in reserves to safeguard some $600 billion in deposits. Privately financed insurers, such as the Securities Investor Protection Corp., are similarly vulnerable to any massive defaults. SIPC, which was created by Congress to protect customers at securities firms registered with the Securities & Exchange Commission, covers brokerage-house accounts of up to $500,000. In addition, most brokers provide additional private insurance, often up to $2 million or more, through arrangements with such companies as Aetna Life & Casualty Co. and Prudential Insurance Co.

As the debt pileup continues, however, the capacity of insurer groups—governmental as well as private—to avert deep trouble becomes increasingly inadequate. "A breakdown of the insurance machinery would be the financial equivalent of nuclear catastrophe," says Albert M. Wojnilower, chief economist of First Boston Corp., and "no individual acting alone can do anything to prevent such a disaster or to protect himself against destruction."[6] Moreover, there are no private incentives to take precautionary measures. Overborrowing, like overspending, has placed us all in a precarious position from which, as we will now explore, painless extrication seems impossible.

Chapter 8

Beyond Our Means

How will it end? Where does our postwar extravagance, our increasing propensity to live beyond our means, finally lead us? And how should we manage our affairs so as best to cope with whatever troubles lie ahead?

Economics isn't really the dismal science as Carlyle suggested. More accurately, as we noted in Chapter 4, it has become the hopeful science. Its practitioners carry on their trade in the hope that through adroit economic management, prosperity can somehow be engendered and preserved. In this belief, the various schools—fiscalist, monetarist, supply-side, and whatever else—all strive to implement their particular prescriptions.

These labors, despite the failures of theory, may not be entirely in vain. Fiscal stimulation assuredly has served from time to time to spur economic activity. The Federal Reserve's sporadic efforts to attune monetary growth to the economy's capacity to expand have surely proved beneficial on occasion. There's clearly something to be said for supply-side measures that may encourage, even slightly, sound entrepreneurial endeavor.

Such considerations must be weighed, however, against the larger fact that we have lived now for too long far beyond our means. We have overborrowed and overconsumed and overpaid ourselves, and all the while we have been investing far too little in the machinery and brick and mortar that ultimately must accompany whatever economic progress we may manage to achieve in coming years. The fault lies not with any particular brand of economics but in our American tendency to live the good life whenever and wherever possible. What remains to be considered is the road ahead, what to expect now.

There's no tidy answer, only a general sense of the eventualities, and it rests not so much on economics as on simple common sense. In brief, the jig is about up and, for all the accumulated wisdom of all the eminent economists of the various schools, painless extrication from our predicament just isn't going to be possible. To be sure, the economic bind that now grips us will be broken in time—perhaps far less of it than anyone now imagines—but only through an intense amount of economic dislocation and downright pain. Just what degree of pain is unclear, but it will arrive, one way or another.

However the bind is broken—through inflation or deflation or otherwise—living standards will suffer, in some households more than in others. Unemployment will mount. Most importantly, financial obligations will be disregarded on a massive scale, for there will be no orderly way to liquidate debts. Perhaps this will happen through default of debt at all levels. Perhaps it will occur through currency debasement during a time of rapidly accelerating inflation. Or perhaps it will happen as a result of crisis legislation, such as a decision to repay Treasury securities coming due at considerably less than full value. Any one of these tactics, or possibly some combination, would be sufficient to erase much or all of the awesome burden of debt that has accumulated in the postwar era and that now presses down on us.

LET'S now examine the various scenarios that could unfold. The least painful is also, unhappily, the least likely—that we pull in our belts and begin living, for the first time in a long time, within our means. Government spending is reined in at long last. Taxes are increased sufficiently to narrow and eventually eliminate the federal-budget deficit. At the same time, the Federal Reserve adeptly channels monetary growth within a narrow range of steady increases consistent with the economy's long-term capacity to expand. These fiscal and monetary restraints, moreover, are undertaken with such surgical precision that business activity continues to rise, not sharply, but at a sustained, healthy pace. No recession threatens. Inflation holds at a minimal level. And yet— *mirabile dictu!*—debt continues to be repaid in a timely manner, by foreign as well as domestic borrowers.

Would that such circumstances could come about. They surely cannot. The business cycle is rooted in human nature, and that is not about to change. Recessions will keep arriving. And there are other questions. How is so much debt, contracted at such high rates of interest, ever to be repaid if inflation remains low? How are double-digit interest charges ever to be serviced by borrowers if the dollar's value no longer depreciates at anything close to the double-digit rates that prevailed when many such loans were first negotiated? How is economic growth to be sustained perennially if the thrust of fiscal and monetary policy is to be relatively restrictive—as it clearly would have to be to reduce and ultimately eliminate all the budgetary red ink? Regarding the nation's other massive deficit—the multibillion-dollar shortfall in foreign trade—how do we regain a competitive stance when, as we've seen, our pay levels far exceed those elsewhere, in some instances by amounts so enormous that even a massive devaluation of the dollar's international exchange value wouldn't help appreciably? And how can we seriously expect relief from protectionist measures, given the impact of the Smoot-Hawley tariff in the Great Depression?

The reality is that our economy today is in many ways far more vulnerable to major disruption than was the case even in 1929, when the depression struck. For one thing, the dimensions of debt in 1929 in many respects were considerably less fearsome than they are now. Today, the U.S. is a debtor nation. It owes more to foreigners than they owe it. And the likelihood is that the imbalance will grow sharply.

C. Fred Bergsten, director of the Institute for International Economics in Washington, estimates that by the end of 1985, the U.S. became "the largest debtor country in the world," and that by 1989 its debt to foreigners "could exceed the total external debt of all the developing countries." In this scenario, America's debt-to-export ratio would exceed 200 percent—the approximate point at which developing countries traditionally have failed to service their external debt—from 1988 onward.[1] In 1929, in contrast, Uncle Sam was an international creditor. Indeed, as we've observed, 1985 marked the first year since World War I in which the U.S. was on balance a debtor.

The matter of third world indebtedness also presents a far more serious difficulty now than in 1929. This is not to say that the less-developed nations were in appreciably sounder financial health then than now. During the Great Depression, several countries in South America, for example, failed to service their international loans. The distinction between now and 1929, however, is that there are so many more developing nations now. Much of what now is labeled the third world was merely a colonial adjunct of industrial Europe in 1929. Much of Africa, for instance, was a colonial part of Britain, France, and Belgium. Accordingly, the debt-repayment problem that now pervades the African continent simply didn't apply in 1929. Where there were colonies in 1929, there now are dozens of newly independent black governments—poor, with mismanaged economies, politically fragile, saddled with failed industrialization programs and unserviceable debt.

In other respects, the international picture is darker now than when the Depression set in. A major factor in the considerable post-World War II growth of economies in general —not simply the U.S. economy—has been the remarkable proliferation of international commerce and investment flows. In the postwar U.S., foreign-trade volume has amounted to larger and larger fractions of overall business activity. A similar pattern of expansion is apparent in investment flows. And the same pattern is evident abroad. As a result, the economies of the world have become ever more tightly linked. Enormous advances in international transportation and communications have spurred the trend. In 1929, in contrast, there was far less economic interdependence. While there is much to applaud in the postwar pattern, it means that when economic trouble now strikes in one place or another around the globe, the repercussions will be more intensely felt than years ago.

Such considerations also raise a question about the Federal Reserve's ability to guide the money supply judiciously. We've seen that the money supply was allowed to contract severely as banks failed in the Great Depression's early stages, a contraction that Nobel laureate Milton Friedman maintains was largely responsible for the slump's ultimate severity. The common assumption now is that the Fed, having learned from the experience of the 1930s, would not again permit such a monetary contraction, however many banks or other thrift institutions may fail.

This no doubt is a sound estimate of the Fed's intentions. But the Fed now faces difficulties on the international front that have no precedent. The country's money supply can no longer be viewed in the sort of isolated perspective implicit in Friedman's critique of policy in the 1930s. The world's new economic interdependence goes hand in hand with a new high degree of interdependence on the monetary front. But questions abound. Is monetary restraint abroad a major reason why, in the 1984–85 business slowdown, or so-called growth recession, the Fed's clearly stimulative monetary policy was so ineffective in fostering a prompt pickup in business activity within the U.S.? Is monetary stimulation by the Fed when the U.S. has a huge trade deficit, as of late, a very different matter from monetary stimulation when, as in the early 1930s, no such shortfall exists? Uncertainty can breed miscalculation. I suspect that the Fed's margin of safety is no broader now than in 1929, only different. And no one knows for sure just where these differences lie.

IF a painless resolution of our difficulties is not possible—and that seems the outlook—what are the likelier scenarios? How will the predicament be resolved?

The most frequently mentioned resolution—but in my view not a very probable one—is the so-called hyperinflation scenario. The German experience with runaway inflation in the 1920s is but one precedent. Austria and France, among other European nations, also were deeply afflicted by runaway inflation in the pre-World War II period. The late E. W. Kemmerer, a Princeton University economist, observed in *The Wall Street Journal* as long ago as 1941 that "economically speaking," it's always possible to wipe out debt by other means, but "politically, inflation is the line of least resistance" when an economy is overburdened by debt and unable, for whatever reasons, to achieve rates of productivity advance sufficiently high to foster sound growth. The horrendous German case shows that the hyperinflationary resolution can be remarkably painless for a very long time; German unemployment held below 4 percent of the labor force until as late as mid-1923. But we've also witnessed that eventually, as a depreciating currency ceases to perform its transactional function, severe economic dislocations develop. In Germany, as a result, joblessness in late 1923 reached even higher levels than those prevailing at the pit of our own deflationary slump in the early 1930s.

The German experience shows how an economy can sink even though inflation, not deflation, pervades the marketplace. Even by comparison with the severe inflationary bouts of the post-World War II era, Germany's inflation of the early 1920s remains awesome. In August 1922, the country's money supply came to 252 billion marks, and by January 1923 it approximated 2 trillion marks. By September of that year, it was up to 28 quadrillion, and a short two months later, it reached 497 quintillion—the number 497 followed by eighteen zeroes.

In late 1923, just before the final collapse of the mark, some German companies were paying their employees with special scrip that could be used to purchase the particular concern's products. Borrowing, not surprisingly, became virtually impossible, as more and more lenders feared they would be repaid in worthless notes, no matter how high the interest rate. Food riots erupted in cities, and prices changed, literally, by the hour. At the beginning of 1922, for instance, the wholesale price index was 4,626 times its 1913 average; by December of the same year, it was 374,563,426,600 times the 1913 level.

As the currency collapsed, business activity slowed sharply. Remarkably, only 3.5 percent of Germany's trade-union members were without jobs as late as July 1923, less than the jobless rate of 6 percent three years earlier, when prices were just starting to climb. But as things deteriorated near the end of 1923 and barter replaced the mark as the main means of conducting trade, unemployment began to leap—to 9.9 percent in September 1923. By year's end, the rate reached 28.2 percent, higher even than the U.S. jobless rate in the worst months of the Depression.

As Germany's runaway inflation worsened, workmanship deteriorated. An index of quality for various products, published in a German newspaper of the day, dropped from a level of 1.00 in April 1921 to 0.82 in October 1922 to 0.64 in October 1923. Only after the old mark became worthless and was replaced in 1924 by a new so-called rentenmark did quality begin to improve again; the index reached 1.24 in April 1924. There was also a tendency, as inflation worsened, toward greater economic concentration. Larger companies gobbled up smaller ones. Fearing shortages, companies that produced consumer goods sought mergers with companies that provided the raw materials required to manufacture such goods.

On an individual level, the inflation brought a greater concentration of personal wealth. Investors with sufficient financial sophistication to anticipate the worsening price spiral were able to hedge much more effectively against it than the middle class, the poor, or older persons on fixed incomes. At the same time, crime proliferated. An index of crimes committed stood at 136 percent of the 1882 average in 1921; by 1923, it was at 170 percent. Crimes committed by young men rocketed to 212 percent of the 1882 average. But once the price spiral broke, the crime rate subsided, even though joblessness remained painfully high.[2]

The sort of hyperinflation that could develop in the U.S. would differ significantly from the German variety of the early 1920s, though there is no reason to suppose that it would prove any less excruciating. The German inflation derived almost entirely, as we've seen, from a soaring money supply that eventually rendered the currency worthless. The sort of hyperinflation that could erupt in the U.S. within the next few years—and by hyperinflation we mean yearly rates of price increase at least in the high double-digit range— would also stem in part from explosive monetary expansion. In addition, however, it would derive from a further sharp increase in the buildup of debt. Borrowing, much of it unwise and not repayable, permeates today's American economy to a far greater degree than it did Germany's economy in the early 1920s.

How could hyperinflation develop in the U.S. between now and, say, the end of this decade? How likely is it?

To tackle the last question first, I would give it a probability rating of perhaps 20 percent. As to the reasons, we've seen that much of the debt suffusing today's economy is of questionable quality and unlikely to be repaid—at least in money that's worth anything remotely close to the value of today's dollar. This applies to debt owed U.S. banks by overextended third world countries, to debt owed American and foreign investors by the U.S. government, to debt owed U.S. mortgage lenders by homeowners, farmers, and business enterprises of countless variety. Much of this debt simply cannot —will not—be repaid in anything like the currency value that lenders anticipated when the loans originally were negotiated.

However, it's possible that overextended borrowers could handle their debt-servicing obligations if they could repay in vastly cheaper dollars. The dollar's value, of course, hinges to a large extent on supply-and-demand forces. Thus, the Federal Reserve has the power to drive down its value by flooding the economy—and indeed the world, since the dollar is a global currency—with money. One incentive would be to help the Treasury service its huge debt burden. Another would be to facilitate the various rescue operations that such other federal agencies as the FDIC appear likely to face. These agencies clearly lack sufficient resources to bail out on their own all the depositors likely to be hurt, for instance, by bank failures. The Federal Reserve, however, can create money out of thin air, as we've seen, and channel it to the FDIC, the FSLIC, or whomever. This can balloon the money supply unless the Fed takes offsetting action in its open-market dealings—for example, by selling Treasury securities in great volume. Perhaps not under Paul Volcker, but surely under a more politically attuned Fed chairman, the Fed may simply decide that ballooning the money supply—and thereby chancing runaway inflation—represents the least painful way to try to cope with deepening economic trouble.

The reason that I regard this inflationary scenario as only a 20 percent possibility involves the somewhat enigmatic role that financial markets have come to play in today's business scene. For a very long time, through much of the 1970s and earlier, lenders were remarkably slow to perceive that future inflation eventually flowed from excessive monetary growth. As a result, many found themselves charging borrowers rates of interest appreciably lower than the rate at which the dollar was losing its value on account of inflation; in economic jargon, real interest rates were negative. This misperception on the part of lenders occurred, I believe, because inflation was minimal through the early postwar period. As for borrowers, I expect that the subsequent degree of inflation constituted a very pleasant surprise.

In any event, many lenders now are spooked. Burned badly in the 1970s, many now are reluctant to lend funds in the fear that inflation may return to torrid levels. And this attitude, I expect, will severely limit the degree to which the Fed can in fact pursue a highly expansionary monetary policy. Let's suppose that the Fed, for reasons elaborated above, begins expanding the money supply at annual rates in the 20-to-30 percent range. Before very long, I imagine, lenders would begin demanding higher and higher interest rates; some might decide not to lend at all. This behavior, in turn, would act to hobble economic activity since, along with money, credit is the lubricant that allows business activity to proceed. The economy, in such a situation, could lurch into precisely the sort of deep slump that government officials would be trying to avoid. I'm convinced that Fed officials are acutely aware of this possibility and, as a result, simply will not attempt to pump up the money supply indefinitely as a way to ease the debt burden.

THIS brings us to the next possible scenario—deflation. I would assign deflation a likelihood of perhaps 30 percent. Deflation is what the U.S. experienced in the 1930s. Prices actually go down when deflation strikes; it's not to be confused with disinflation, a far less painful circumstance, under which inflation merely abates, as happened in 1983–84.

How can deflation occur if the Federal Reserve is unwilling to allow the sort of shrinkage of the money supply that took place in the early 1930s? The answer is that shaky loans have become so pervasive nowadays that eventually spreading defaults and bankruptcies may simply overwhelm the Fed's capacity to offset the tendency of the money supply to contract as institutions fail on a massive scale. If a balloon has only a couple of holes in it, you may keep it inflated by vigorously pumping in air; the inflow will counterbalance the outflow. But when there are a dozen or more holes in the balloon and new ones are appearing every few seconds, even vigorous pumping may not provide a sufficient inflow to prevent its collapse.

Let's suppose that bank failures increase so rapidly that the Fed simply can't move swiftly enough—independently or through such other agencies as the FDIC—to perform the necessary amount of bailing out. In such a situation, the money supply would tend to contract, perhaps even more sharply than in the Depression. A contracting money supply would surely lead to falling prices, mounting joblessness and, in the end, an economic environment similar to that of the 1930s.

How, precisely, might the Fed be overwhelmed? Let's imagine that in a single week not only Continental Illinois but a dozen large banks can't honor their financial commitments. Perhaps the Fed would be able to supply reserves in sufficient quantity and quickly enough to keep the banks in business, but that's by no means a sure thing. The aforementioned difficulties at thrift institutions in Maryland and Ohio —infinitesimal in terms of what is imagined here—provide scant assurance that the Fed, or any other governmental agency, would in fact ride to the rescue in timely fashion in the event of a really widespread financial collapse. Could the monetary authorities possibly cope, for example, if a wave of third world repudiations happened to hit simultaneously with a new rash of loan defaults by oil-drilling companies and farmers? I doubt it.

The already precarious nature of the agricultural situation

is evident in a government study made in late 1985 that shows deep trouble within the Federal Farm Credit System. The system, which holds more than $60 billion in loans to farmers and ranchers, could well collapse, according to the analysis. It questions whether the system has been writing off bad loans promptly and finds the system's capital structure exceedingly shaky. The system constitutes the country's largest single credit source for farmers and ranchers. It operates twelve regional banks, each with three lending arms: an intermediate credit bank, a land bank for farmland loans, and a bank for farm cooperatives.

In early 1985, the system's only really liquid asset was some $3.4 billion held in the form of securities. Yet the system had over $60 billion in debt outstanding—mainly in the form of publicly sold bonds and notes. These bonds and notes, I should add, are not federally guaranteed, despite a widespread notion to the contrary, and the interest payments due on them depend on the capacity of agricultural borrowers to service their own debt. As we've seen, that capacity is highly suspect. In the third quarter of 1985, the system sustained a $522.3 million loss because of the failure of farmers to repay loans. This compared with a net gain of $126.4 million a year earlier. For all of 1985, the system lost an estimated $2.7 billion, which was covered by some $11 billion that the system had in reserves, partly as a result of emergency legislation allowing the system when in difficulty to tap special funds at the Treasury. By mid-1986, these reserves were below $6 billion and the full-year loss was expected to approximate $2 billion.

The deflation scenario also takes into account the distressing mathematics of debt compounding. Taken as a whole, public and private debt in the U.S. now exceeds $7 trillion and, through the magic of compounding, that figure could easily double by the end of this decade if present trends persist. Looking further ahead, total debt could well reach some $57 trillion by 1995 and, again through compounding,

$448 trillion by 2015. It's unreasonable to suppose that the Fed or any other governmental or private institution could contain the trouble that would inevitably arise in such a debt-burdened future.

"The Fed assumes that it can always make money fast enough to avert a deflationary collapse such as was seen in the 1930s, but it is highly questionable whether the Fed can create money fast enough to overcome the compounding factor," warns Julian Snyder of *International Moneyline.* Snyder maintains that "all it would take [for deflation] would be for several large financial institutions and corporations to fail simultaneously in the Ohio pattern; the Fed could stop a run on a single bank, but it would be impossible to stop a run on several banks at the same time."

The role of compounding is apparent, among other places, in the federal debt situation. Interest obligations on the federal debt are rising faster than national income can possibly expand each year, and national income of course ultimately supplies federal revenues. This means that interest costs must rise as a percentage of national income. Let's assume that the average interest rate on federal debt outstanding is 12 percent and that additional federal borrowing will also be financed at 12 percent. Let's also assume that future growth of national income is expected to average 9 percent annually, of which 5 to 6 percent will represent simply inflation. These assumptions are all reasonably close to the actual outlook foreseen by many economists in 1985. Under these circumstances, income would double every eight years, while federal debt would double every six years. Looking further ahead, income would double three times in the next twenty-four years, but debt would double four times. In the process, the federal budget deficit would rise with recent trends from 4 percent of gross national product, where it has ranged of late, to about 8 percent, and the national debt would rise from about one third of GNP to two thirds. "The arithmetic of deficit finance becomes rather dismal," remarks Jerry L. Jordan, the former presidential adviser.

The swelling debt burden is by no means the only consideration in the deflationary scenario. The price of oil is another. Robert Horton, managing director of British Petroleum Corp., touched on this concern when he warned an oil industry conference in London in mid-1985 that a prolonged "collapse in the oil price would trigger a major financial crisis, requiring the Federal Reserve to launch a lifeboat the size of the QE 2." Even if the Fed were able to launch such a lifeboat, there surely would be lengthy bureaucratic and legislative delays, perhaps covering weeks. Again, deflation could threaten.

THE reason I've assigned the deflation scenario no more than a 30 percent probability, however, is that I'm convinced such gloomy forecasters as Julian Snyder—and he is only one of many deflationists—tend to underestimate Washington's power.[3] I believe that there's a 50 percent chance that our economy will avoid both hyperinflation and the sort of severe, prolonged deflation outlined above, and instead will enter a new era of intensifying governmental regulation over the economy. This may seem a peculiar forecast when a leading conservative occupies the Oval Office at the White House and when the Republican party appears to be winning converts from the Democratic ranks. Yet a highly regimented economy is precisely where we are most likely to wind up as a result of our efforts to deregulate, particularly in the financial markets, and to pare taxes and in general unleash free enterprise. Not immediately, perhaps, but very possibly before this decade is out.

How might all this happen?

My guess is that first off, the economy will lapse into yet another recession that perhaps will arrive before the end of Reagan's second term, which expires in January 1989. That certainly is what experience suggests, as we've seen earlier in our discussion of the business cycle. Because of the rigidities and excesses that have built up over the postwar era and that now permeate our economy, the next recession will quickly deepen. Business failures will rapidly mount; even now, after more than three years of economic growth, corporate balance sheets by and large are lamentably feeble. Unemployment will rapidly return to the double-digit range that briefly was reached in the 1981–82 recession. Banks and other thrift institutions will be unable to carry out their financial obligations to an extent that will make today's sporadic difficulties seem almost inconsequential. The federal-budget deficit will swiftly worsen as revenues diminish; this will complicate governmental efforts to stimulate a sagging economy.

Deflation will be beckoning, to be sure. But I don't believe that it will really settle in, at least not for very long. And not because the Fed will be pumping up the money supply at a swift pace—which, I expect, it will be doing to a degree. Deflation, as it occurred during the Great Depression, won't take hold because the government, however reluctantly at first, will be stepping in across the entire economic landscape —not just through the Fed. It will step in gingerly perhaps at the beginning, but then more and more boldly as the recession deepens and the 1988 presidential election nears. Democrats by then will be gaining political strength amid the shambles of a Republican policy that disregarded a most basic lesson of this century's economic history: that the sort of laissez-faire, unregulated business environment that was evolving by the mid-1980s was precisely the sort of environment that existed—notwithstanding the distinctions—in 1929.

As long ago as the 1970s, Albert Wojnilower of First Boston lamented the pattern of financial deregulation—for instance, the progressive removal of various interest-rate ceilings— that was beginning to transform U.S. financial markets and banking and has been spurred by Reaganites. "Recent strains in the banking system," Wojnilower now says, "are the inevitable result of deregulation." To prevent a worsening situation, he urges, "we should, among other things, restore some banking regulations, particularly limits on deposit interest." In return for accepting relatively low rates, he recalls, the public got sound deposit insurance and sound banks. Higher interest rates may be tempting, but, he adds in an understatement, that "confidence in the banking system isn't what it used to be." As he says, deregulation in banking, as well as elsewhere, has led to "excessive credit expansion and bankruptcy risk [and] has already spawned a series of crises and will cause more."

The governmental impetus in the next recession to reregulate is unlikely to stop with the banking industry. I expect that foreign trade will come under much tighter supervision. A *Business Week* poll in 1985 found that most Americans already favor added curbs against imports, especially those emanating from Japan.[4] My guess is that U.S. trade policy will become increasingly protectionist as the next recession deepens and, initially if not in the long run, this may help save some U.S. factory jobs. Protectionism was also a factor in the Democrats' regaining control of the Senate in 1986.

By the time the 1988 election rolls around, as New York investment banker Felix Rohatyn has put it, "we may be looking for another Franklin Roosevelt to pull the country together in a time of great economic and social stress." Rohatyn is on the mark when he notes the irony that "a policy intended to reduce to a minimum the level of government involvement in the economy would have created a situation in which such government involvement would have to return to its highest level since 1932."[5]

MY own view is that the involvement level, once the Democrats return to the White House in 1989, may well be higher than in the New Deal and later. This, it seems to me, is the likely Reagan legacy. But it's not his legacy only. It's the legacy of a postwar era in which dreams, to be sure, were realized, in which living standards rose from year to year, in which a belief prevailed that a 1930s debacle just couldn't happen again and interrupt the good life.

As the government becomes ever more deeply involved in the economy's workings, in the marketplace, how will the various difficulties now confronting us be resolved? How will the oppressive burden of debt be lifted? How will the budget deficit be narrowed?[6] How will the banks be rescued as borrowers by the millions fail to service their obligations?

My guess is that government debt will be repaid—and the deficit effectively erased—in a manner tantamount to default —or confiscation. Holders of Treasury securities coming due may be told, for instance, that unless their bills, notes, or bonds are rolled over, Uncle Sam will pay only a specified fraction of face value. Interest payments on such securities may also be capped. This would amount, of course, to repudiation of a large part of the federal debt and would require legislative action. But that could come swiftly under such dire conditions. Nationalization of the banking system would no doubt be a part of the operation. As long ago as October 1984, William Isaac of the FDIC warned a New York banking group of the need for "greater market discipline" in banking and suggested that Uncle Sam might eventually have to supply the restraining influence through outright control of the institutions.

Our main matter of concern, then, isn't hyperinflation or deflation but the prospect of greatly increased governmental control over all aspects of economic activity. This is what the future seems to hold. And we shouldn't be overly surprised. After all, if one looks back not just a few decades but over the centuries, increasing governmental involvement in economic affairs is an overriding pattern. The recent years of freer and freer markets may well be remembered a decade hence as only a pleasant but foolish interlude—an aberration —in a transcendent long-term trend.

In the sort of business climate that could well emerge, the Federal Reserve Board could lose its present independence and be placed under the firm thumb of the White House. All banks, indeed all thrift institutions, could wind up being nationalized. Foreign trade and capital transactions most likely would be government managed. Wages and prices would largely be set by people in Washington. Tax rates would be far higher than now and enforcement far stricter. Corporate managers would be under rigid governmental supervision that would make today's regulations seem blissfully relaxed.

All in all a new era would be upon us, a far less carefree one, whose roots trace back to the earlier decades of overindulgence. It's not a cheerful prospect, but it's a likely one.

How can investors protect themselves if this scenario does unfold? There's really little that can be done. If hyperinflation were the likeliest prospect, one could readily hedge against it by investing in such tangibles as gold and real estate. If deflation were highly probable, bonds of top-rated companies and even cash would be in order. But the prospect of spreading governmental control over the economy— over our lives—is another matter. Black markets become more attractive, of course. The so-called underground economy—off-the-books transactions, which may actually have diminished in recent years with the reduction in tax rates— receives a new life. Legally, however, there's little that individual investors can do to protect themselves against an encroaching Washington presence. Legislation is always unpredictable, but luck and pull in the federal power centers become supremely important. One can seek a freer investment climate abroad if international investing is allowed, which is doubtful. But where to invest abroad? The next recession won't be limited to these shores but will spread and in the process spur the growth of government regulation abroad as at home.

The best investment, under such circumstances, will be in one's affiliations. Individuals employed by large, powerful organizations with governmental ties and clout will surely fare far better than the self-employed person who hopes to build enduring financial independence through hard work and ingenuity.

The dream of the Reagan years and earlier—that we can go on indefinitely living beyond our means—will at last be dead as the government extends its influence. Uncle Sam will be everywhere, and a key to investment success will be one's ability to bend or circumvent the rules and traverse the underground economy.

The Reagan goal of uninhibited self-help and self-interest will be a memory. But we will have begun, for the first time in a very long time, to live within our means—under much duress and not nearly as comfortably as we might have done had the proper belt-tightening been undertaken decades ago. But that's another story, one that sadly never happened.

Notes

Introduction

1. For a gripping account of the 1938 hurricane, there is none better than Everett S. Allen's *A Wind to Shake the World,* published in 1976 by Little, Brown & Co. At the time of the big blow, Allen was a new reporter for the New Bedford *Standard-Times* and covered it for the paper. He went on to become the paper's chief editorial writer. He calls the 1938 hurricane the worst natural disaster in American history.

Chapter 1: On Borrowed Time

1. The long rise of debt, in its various manifestations, can best be glimpsed perhaps in the Federal Reserve Board's *Historical Chart Book,* published monthly and in annual supplements and available through the Government Printing Office as well as the Federal Reserve Board in Washington.

2. The rise of transfer payments is documented, among other places, in various Commerce Department publications, including notably the agency's monthly *Survey of Current Business.* This fine publication also is a primary source for a great many other statistics, ranging from data on debt and spending, discussed in this chapter, to an assortment of statistics that bear on the country's international transactions.

3. Michael Boskin, a Stanford University economist, reckons in his excellent book *The Uncertain Future of Social Security* that when the so-called baby boomers start retiring in 2020, there will be fifty Social Security recipients for every one hundred workers. He further estimates that over the next seventy-five years, the gap between revenues and benefits will be on the order of $1.6 trillion, very roughly the size of the present national debt. He regards a 1983 "rescue" plan for Social Security as woefully inadequate.

4. These calculations are based on a February 1985 study by Martin Lefkowitz, director of economic trends and statistics for the U.S. Chamber of Commerce in Washington.

5. The generosity of military benefits is reviewed in a March 1985 report by the Center on Budget and Policy Priorities, a private organization that studies trends in federal spending.

6. These individuals and others are described in an article in the March 7, 1985, issue of the New York *Daily News.*

7. These and other findings are contained in a study reported in the December 10, 1984, issue of *U.S. News & World Report.*

8. Here and elsewhere in this book, a primary source of labor-force data is the Labor Department's excellent publication, *The Monthly Labor Review.*

9. Savings and income data, like that on debt and spending, is a Commerce Department responsibility and may be followed, among other places, in the *Survey of Current Business.*

Chapter 2: Borrow and Buy

1. Loan delinquencies are tracked regularly by the American Bankers Association and the Mortgage Bankers Association of America.

2. For an authoritative discussion of the Federal Reserve's unfortunate squeezing of the money supply in this period, there is no better report than that contained in Chapter Seven of *A Monetary History of the United States,* by Milton Friedman and Anna Schwartz, published by the National Bureau of Economic Research.

3. Such data are contained, among other places, in the Federal Reserve's aforementioned *Historical Chart Book.*

4. Extensive research on this matter has been conducted by Robert Gough, an economist on the staff of Data Resources Inc., as well as by Alan Greenspan, president of Townsend-Greenspan Co.

5. Estimates of factory operating levels, here and elsewhere, are based on regular calculations by the Federal Reserve Board.

Chapter 3: The Gap Goes On

1. Besides frequent Labor Department analyses of the labor-cost situation, a particularly excellent report is that issued in August 1985 by the Economic Services unit of New York's Citicorp.

2. These data derive from a study published in 1985 by Union Bank of Switzerland.

3. This particular survey was conducted in September 1985 by Towers, Perrin, Forster & Crosby, the management consultants. Other such surveys by other organizations show a similar pattern.

4. An excellent report on union membership in the major industrial nations is the March 1985 study by the Conference Board.

5. This analysis, by Robert Crandall, is contained in the Summer 1984 issue of *The Brookings Review.*

Chapter 4: Nothing Works

1. This comment was made during a fund-raising speech that Will gave in New York before prospective donors (including me) for his alma mater, Trinity College, of Hartford, Connecticut. Although I was a member of his audience, as an editor in the *Journal's* news department rather than its editorial page, I made no response to his indictment of the paper. I felt that if any answering back was in order, it should be done by the paper's editorial-page writers, who had championed the supply-side cause from the start.

Chapter 5: The Enduring Cycle

1. The ups and downs of the business cycle are recorded in *Business Conditions Digest,* a monthly publication of the Commerce Department, and it is must reading for serious students of the economy's progress and history. Like most such publications, it is available through the Government Printing Office.

2. Analysts at Columbia University's Center for International Business Cycle Research received $150,000 from the Alfred P. Sloan Foundation in 1986 to find ways in which the Commerce Department may improve the reliability of its various indicators. The research is expected to be completed by the end of 1987.

3. Of many fine studies of Kondratieff theory, one of the best in recent years appeared as a long cover story in the November 9, 1981, issue of *Forbes* magazine.

Chapter 6: Spending Rolls On

1. Stein's article appeared in the paper on March 12, 1984. Since then, the world has grown ever more dangerous for Americans, yet the nation's military programs remain a primary target of budget-cutting advocates.

2. Stockman continued to receive heavy criticism after moving into a lucrative investment-banking job on Wall Street. When his book, titled *The Triumph of Politics: Why the Reagan Revolution Failed,* appeared in the spring of 1986, it was widely panned as a misguided complaint over an economic policy that had actually worked well. Yet the federal budget was in deeper deficit then than when Reagan was first settling into the White House. Stockman was a man ahead of his time.

3. While attending a hockey game at New York's Madison Square Garden in May 1986, which was won by his beloved Rangers, Grace ruefully conceded to me that "nothing really has been or is being done" in Washington to implement his commission's many recommendations.

Chapter 7: Debt Rolls On

1. The deteriorating situation is described well by Charles F. McCoy in a front-page *Wall Street Journal* report, titled "Loan Morass," in the issue of December 2, 1985.

2. Two excellent recapitulations of Continental's fall appeared on the front pages of *The Wall Street Journal*—"Banker Uncle Sam" on July 19, 1984, and "Anatomy of Failure" on July 30, 1984.

3. Huston's remarkable ability to retain the respect of his fellow Iowans even while he was closing their banks is documented by Marj Charlier in *The Wall Street Journal* of June 11, 1985.

4. The Schlesinger interview with Castro appeared on *The Wall Street Journal's* editorial page on June 12, 1985.

5. Throughout this period, the economy remained in an expansionary phase of the business cycle, and so there was really no test of the worrisome thesis that junk bonds lead to major trouble once a recession develops.

6. Wojnilower, in my view, is the most articulate, as well as one of the very brightest, of Wall Street's many economists. These particular remarks of his were delivered in October 1985 in Florence, Italy, before a conference on "The Origins and Diffusion of Financial Innovation."

Chapter 8: Beyond Our Means

1. Bergsten's scenario was laid out in extensive detail in a speech that he delivered on February 27, 1985, in London, before the Confederation of British Industries.

2. Possibly the best source of economic data on the German hyperinflation is that contained in an exhaustive 1931 study of the debacle by the Italian economist Constantino Bresciani-Turroni. Another good source is a book titled *Exchange, Prices and Production in Hyper-Inflation: Germany 1920–23*, by an American economist at Princeton University, Frank D. Graham.

3. The most persistent deflationist, perhaps, is John Exter, an investment adviser based in New Jersey, whose earlier career included stints at Citicorp and within the Federal Reserve System. I have known John for about twenty-five years and for twenty-five years he has been warning me that prices would collapse.

4. The poll appeared in the April 8, 1985, issue under the heading: "Resentment of Japan Is Deepening," which indeed has been happening, though quite unfairly, in my opinion; they work harder, save more, and spend more carefully.

5. Rohatyn set down his concerns at length in the March 29, 1984, issue of *The New York Review of Books*. As a partner of the investment-banking firm of Lazard Frères & Co., he also could appreciate—and enjoy—the enormous financial gains accruing to such firms as his own under Reagan's leadership in Washington.

6. Robert Eisner, a Northwestern University economist, maintains in his recent book *How Real Is The Federal Deficit?* that the enormous federal debt and deficits derive largely from accounting techniques that exaggerate red ink. But his adjusted data still show a distressing picture.

Index

ALFRED L. MALABRE, JR., has covered the ups and downs of the U.S. economy for *The Wall Street Journal* for three decades. He also has written three earlier books on the subject, including the widely acclaimed *Understanding the Economy: For People Who Can't Stand Economics.* Educated at St. Paul's School in Concord, New Hampshire, and Yale University, Malabre's first job in journalism, after a four-year stint in the U.S. Navy during the Korean War, was with the *Hartford Courant.* Before becoming economics news editor of the *Journal* in 1969, he served in the *Journal's* London and Bonn bureaus and was chief of the latter. He is also an author of the paper's front-page Monday morning column "The Outlook." He lives in Manhattan with his wife, Patricia, and two Shetland sheep dogs.